Praise

"Natalie Snapp takes us on a j[...] brokenness to wholeness, fear t[...] ney she has traveled herself. Natalie beautifully weaves the story of God's grace in the life of Bathsheba with her own story of God's grace while giving us space to find that same grace within our lives. If you're walking through a season of suffering, disappointment, or uncertainty, I encourage you to take Natalie's hand as she leads you to the One who holds your future and your hope."
—**Karina Allen**, life coach, speaker, worship leader/songwriter, and author for Dayspring's (in)courage Community

"Natalie Snapp caused me to think about Bathsheba as I never had before. Considering her circumstances, fears, and relationships brought out her humanity and made her relatable in a fresh way."
—**Melissa Spoelstra**, Bible teacher, speaker, and author of *Romans: Good News That Changes Everything* and numerous other Bible studies and books

"If you have ever felt deeply misunderstood, you may have more in common with Bathsheba than you realize. With grace and wisdom, Natalie Snapp invites you into Bathsheba's story and reveals the heart of a woman who found herself in an impossible situation yet who overcame great adversity with incredible strength. *The Bathsheba Battle* shows us that restoration is what God does best. It's what He did for Bathsheba, and it's what He can do for you."
—**Denise J. Hughes**, author of *Deeper Waters: Immersed in the Life-Changing Truth of God's Word* and general editor for the *CSB (in)courage Devotional Bible*

"Natalie beautifully lifts the story of Bathsheba out of the shadow of the larger story of David, reminding us that the Bible is filled with real people and unedited stories we all can relate to. This book will encourage every woman who has walked through a hard story and found God in the midst of it, loving and redeeming all."
—**Stacey Thacker**, author of *The Girlfriends' Guide to the Bible* series

"In *The Bathsheba Battle*, Natalie shines light on topics we often keep hidden in the dark. With Bathsheba's story as a backdrop, we are invited to consider our response to suffering and move past inclinations of shame, anger, and comparison into the hope and wholeness we have in Christ. For anyone who has experienced

heartache, Natalie's wise words offer a biblically sound path toward healing. And for those who want to come alongside a friend who is suffering, Natalie's gentle manner provides an example of how to love others well. Moving from sorrow to hope isn't an easy journey, but it is an important one for all who want to love well."
—**Teri Lynne Underwood**, author of *Praying for Girls: Asking God for the Things They Need Most*

The Bathsheba Battle

Finding Hope When Life Takes an Unexpected Turn

Natalie Chambers Snapp

ABINGDON PRESS
NASHVILLE

THE BATHSHEBA BATTLE
FINDING HOPE WHEN LIFE TAKES AN UNEXPECTED TURN

Copyright © 2019 Abingdon Press

All rights reserved.

Library of Congress Control Number has been requested.

ISBN 978-1-5018-9080-2

All Scripture quotations, unless otherwise noted, are taken from the Holy Bible, New International Version®, NIV®. Copyright © 1973, 1978, 1984, 2011 by Biblica, Inc.™ Used by Permission of Zondervan. All rights reserved worldwide. www.zondervan.com.

2015 Edition: Scripture quotations taken from the Amplified® Bible (AMP), Copyright © 2015 by The Lockman Foundation. Used by permission. www.Lockman.org.

Scripture quotations are from the ESV® Bible (The Holy Bible, English Standard Version®), copyright © 2001 by Crossway, a publishing ministry of Good News Publishers. Used by permission. All rights reserved.

Scripture quotations marked MSG are taken from THE MESSAGE, copyright © 1993, 1994, 1995, 1996, 2000, 2001, 2002 by Eugene H. Peterson. Used by permission of NavPress. All rights reserved. Represented by Tyndale House Publishers, Inc.

Scripture quotations marked NLV are taken from the New Life Version copyright © 1969 and 2003. Used by permission of Barbour Publishing, Inc., Uhrichsville, Ohio, 44683. All rights reserved.

Scripture quotations marked NLT are taken from the Holy Bible, New Living Translation, copyright ©1996, 2004, 2015 by Tyndale House Foundation. Used by permission of Tyndale House Publishers, Inc., Carol Stream, Illinois 60188. All rights reserved.

19 20 21 22 23 24 25 26 27 28—10 9 8 7 6 5 4 3 2 1
MANUFACTURED IN THE UNITED STATES OF AMERICA

*To every woman who has ever walked through a battle
and emerged more faithful, resilient, and hope-filled:
When I see you, I see the work of God—and it's a beautiful sight to behold.
Keep looking to Him, sisters, and you will never fail.*

*And to the following women who have been through excruciatingly
difficult valleys and have inspired me greatly:*

*Sarah Lenox Quick
Peggy Buchanan
Patty Gates
Mariam Lenox
Nancy Wethington
Michelle Granitz
Karri Huckstep
Jenifer Stuelpe Gibbs*

Contents

Introduction

ello, Fellow Broken-Road Traveler.

I'm so thankful you've picked up this book. We have a lot to talk about. Oh, do we ever.

If we were sitting in a room together and someone asked, "Who would like to experience pain and suffering today?" would you wave your hand high? Who trudges through life's biggest challenges with excitement and joy? Who welcomes hardship? Who willingly walks into life's most difficult situations with anticipation and passion? Certainly not me and—since you're reading this—I suspect certainly not you either.

Maybe you're in need of some healing these days. Life isn't going as planned. Perhaps it has taken a very unexpected turn that has led you right into a deep valley. You want the pain to just go away, and right about now you're wishing there was a fast-forward button you could push to better days ahead. Maybe you're wondering what on earth God is doing in you, through you, and for you. Maybe you've given up, hopelessly throwing your hands in the air and allowing bitterness and anger to just have at it. You desire healing and hope, but instead you feel stuck in your circumstances and disappointments.

Transformation happens during renovation.

If it's any consolation, I've been there, done that, and gotten way more T-shirts than I ever wanted. I also know I will be there again. Pain and suffering are cyclical on this side of heaven. But here's the thing: transformation happens during renovation. And renovation happens when we walk through the valley, sweet sister. The late Reverend Billy Graham once said, "Mountaintops are for views and inspiration, but fruit grows in the valley."[1] Amen, Reverend Graham. No one has ever experienced their most powerful personal growth on the mountaintop. The fruit we grow in the valley leads to the free and full life God wants us to live.

Yet here's the thing: you already know this. You've heard it many times before; but sometimes, knowing the fruit will come is not much help in the everyday struggle just to survive the pain. To steal a popular tagline, life comes at us fast. There are bills to pay. Children to shuffle around. Careers to advance. Meals to prepare. Laundry to do. You know it well. When the unexpected comes and we find ourselves in the valley of pain and suffering, everyday tasks can feel like monumental achievements—because they are. All of this living can lead to a busyness that can distract us temporarily; however, in the still, quiet moments, we can't run. It's in those moments where we have a choice: we can listen to the one who comes "to steal and kill and destroy" or to the One who gives us life "to the full" (John 10:10).

With every valley we tread, we experience that much more freedom and that much less fear.

The thief wants us to stay confused, bitter, angry, and resentful, knowing that if we emerge from this valley victorious then God will be glorified. But the One who is on our side wants new life for us. He knows that with every valley we tread, we experience that much more freedom and that much less fear. Of the many verses on pain and suffering God shares with His followers, the one that offers me the most comfort is this: "He heals the brokenhearted and binds up their wounds" (Psalm 147:3). Let that sink in for a minute. He heals the brokenhearted. Know anything about a broken heart? Doesn't healing sound good right about now? Not only does He heal our broken hearts but also He binds up our wounds. If you cut a gash in your leg, you're going to go to the hospital where they will sew it up and dress the wound so it can heal. Just as the doctor binds your physical wound, God does the same with our internal wounds. He binds them up so they can heal.

According to *Merriam-Webster*, the definition of the word *heal* is "to cause an undesirable condition to be overcome; to patch up or correct a breach or division; or to restore to original purity or integrity."[2] God promises He will cause your undesirable condition to be overcome. He will work to encourage peace when there has been a breach or division. And God is always, always in the business of restoration. In fact, that's pretty much what He's all about. He sent us His Son, Jesus, so our relationship with Him could be restored. That kind of healing is not only impressive, friend. It's astounding.

Before we jump into the heart of this amazing story, I want to let you in on a great feature following each chapter. Since this book will be effective whether you choose to read it alone or with a group, I have included applicable scripture and reflection questions for you to think about and discuss. However, might I add that the benefits of reading this book with a group are huge? When we engage in discussion about content we are reading, especially content such as the life of Bathsheba, we learn so much from the people reading the same information. Studying the Bible is greatly enhanced when we can ask questions, pose thoughts, and share our own personal journey. I strongly encourage you to grab a few friends and read this together.

INTRODUCTION

There is purpose in our suffering. I won't lie; when I used to hear this in the past, it made me want to pull my hair out. Perhaps you feel the same. Yet we find great encouragement in the story of Bathsheba, one of my favorite women of the Bible. She certainly knew what it was like for life to take an unexpected turn. One minute she was minding her own business, taking a bath, and the next her whole world was turned upside down. This woman knew what it was like to walk through the valley of pain and suffering. Yet, despite her suffering, she bore fruit that grew—even while she was at the lowest point of her life.

As we explore Bathsheba's story, along with some practical insights for the journey to healing and wholeness, we'll see that her suffering renovated her into a woman of confidence, wisdom, and love. And best of all, God didn't just do this for Bathsheba. He promises healing and hope for all of us. We just have to be willing to listen to the One who is for us—the One who has come to give us life to the full.

Part 1

Sorting Through the Suffering

Getting Real

> Two roads diverged in a wood, and I—
> I took the one less traveled by,
> And that has made all the difference.
>
> —Robert Frost,
> "The Road Not Taken"

The dryer rumbled with yet another load of laundry, the dogs beckoned to be let outside, and I needed to go to the grocery store, but suddenly overcome with pain, I crumbled to the floor of my closet and cried deep, guttural sobs. Confusion, anger, bitterness, and, yeah, a little entitlement emerged as I told God just what I thought of the recent explosion of so many important relationships in my life. I mean, for crying out loud, I wrote a book about female friendships. But here's the thing: it's not uncommon for us to be attacked in the very areas where we step out in faith to write or speak or teach. As I found myself descending into a valley of emotional pain, I knew I had a choice to make. Which road would I take?

I remember the first time I read Robert Frost's poem "The Road Not Taken." English class, sophomore year of high school. Honestly, in those days I cared more about making sure I had my ClairMist hairspray and who was going to ask me to the homecoming dance; so when something like a poem by Robert Frost yanked me to attention, it had to be good. It is, and I still think of his words often today. Twelve years after first reading Frost's poem, I became a follower of Jesus and started to read the Bible. Imagine my delight when I stumbled upon Matthew 7:13-14: "Enter through the narrow gate. For wide is the gate and broad is the road that leads to destruction, and many enter through it. But small is the gate and narrow the road that leads to life, and only a few find it."

The effort is almost always worth the outcome.

Holy cow. Right there, in the Bible, was exactly what Robert Frost was saying. Frost said he chose the road less taken, and that one choice made all the difference in his life. Likewise, the narrow path, the path few choose, will make all the difference for us. This narrow path leads to life, but only a few of us will find it. The wider path, the path chosen by most, leads to destruction. How do we get on the right path? I wish there was another way, sister, but it's usually when we experience deep pain and suffering that we start to walk the narrow path. In fact, it's almost always pain and suffering that deliver us right to the front doorstep of that path. Our pain and suffering, the very thing none of us wants, is actually the vehicle God uses to invite us to the narrow path—the one where we find life.

Let's face it: the narrow path isn't easy, and that's why few choose to go there. The wider path—the path of least resistance—is usually the more popular choice because it's human nature to choose ease over difficulty. If we are going on a hike, I'm not going to be superexcited to see a narrow path winding up and down steep hills that span many miles. While we're hiking, I might mumble under my breath just how

I'm feeling about that difficult terrain and tell you how over it I am. I sure don't want to see a valley between the hills because that means I have to climb up and down again! Yet we'll build muscle, burn calories, and probably feel pretty good about ourselves when we're finished. We might even tell other people stories about navigating that intense hike and laugh about what we mumbled under our breath when we didn't quite understand the big picture. The fact remains, the effort is almost always worth the outcome.

Here's the other thing about that hike: we will learn just as much, if not more, during the hike than we will have learned when it's over. In other words, the process is just as important, if not more so, than the product. My husband, Jason, and his friend Pedro hiked the Machu Picchu trail ten years ago, and we still hear stories from that trip. There were times they both wanted to strangle one another (Pedro's wife, Nicole, and I are very thankful they didn't!). There were times when they were starving but had to keep going. They were often overcome with physical exhaustion. One night it rained for hours in their tent while they were trying to sleep. Honestly, it sounds horrible when they talk about it. Needless to say, I wasn't exactly booking a trip as soon as I possibly could.

But then I remembered the call I received from Jason just as he ascended to the point where they could see Machu Picchu. With tears streaming down his face, he told me the beauty was unimaginable. They achieved something so few have achieved because most people choose to take the train up to the ruins and get it done in a day. This road less taken led to a victory so sweet, it's something Jason and Pedro will hold dear in their hearts for the rest of their lives. That excruciatingly difficult hike led to a tangible victory that could not be experienced by taking the train.

Something else to note: Jason and Pedro sometimes saw the trains taking the tourists up to the ruins and were a little envious. When we're hiking that rough terrain, we might be tempted to look sideways and start feeling sorry for ourselves because there are some who get to ride the train. Just remember: they get to ride the train at that moment. You will get to ride the train someday too. Your period of suffering will not last forever, and you'll be invited to sit on the train again—and maybe even have a great cup of coffee. And the best part is, when you're on the train, the people who were once on the train and are now hiking might need some encouragement and support. We'll talk about that again soon, but the wisdom we glean while we're on the hike will definitely help others who will hike in the future.

Now, at this point, you may be thinking, "I hate hiking, Natalie. I don't care about seeing the ruins. I just want to get this over with and get on the train." And listen, I know you do. We all do. But something transformational and magical happens when we're hiking that difficult hike: we become more vulnerable. Our vulnerability leads to authenticity, and authenticity leads to trust. Trust leads to contentment, and contentment leads to peace. Peace leads to real, honest-to-goodness joy. Worth it? Absolutely.

One of my favorite books is *The Velveteen Rabbit*. If you aren't familiar with the story, the velveteen rabbit is a stuffed bunny that is the most-loved toy of a young boy. The boy comes down with scarlet fever, and, sadly, his sheets, pillows, blankets, and the bunny have to be burned. Of course, this happens later in the story after we've had plenty of time to love the bunny, so we are just as devastated as the young boy. But guess what happens? When the stuffed bunny is burned, he becomes a real bunny. However, before he becomes a real bunny, he feels a little apprehensive about becoming real. The skin horse, another toy in the toy room, says this:

> "Real isn't how you are made," said the Skin
> Horse. "It's a thing that happens to you. When
> a child loves you for a long, long time, not just

to play with, but REALLY loves you, then you become Real."

"Does it hurt?" asked the Rabbit.

"Sometimes," said the Skin Horse, for he was always truthful. "When you are Real you don't mind being hurt."

"Does it happen all at once, like being wound up," he asked, "or bit by bit?"

"It doesn't happen all at once," said the Skin Horse. "You become. It takes a long time. That's why it doesn't happen often to people who break easily, or have sharp edges, or who have to be carefully kept. Generally, by the time you are Real, most of your hair has been loved off, and your eyes drop out and you get loose in the joints and very shabby. But these things don't matter at all, because once you are Real you can't be ugly, except to people who don't understand."[1]

Sometimes the path to becoming real hurts. It takes time to become. People who break easily or have sharp edges may never become real. By the time you become real, it might show in ways you wish it didn't, but those dark circles under your eyes matter less because it's when we become real that we become free. And freedom comes from only one source: our Creator.

From the moment I first opened my Bible almost twenty years ago, I have been intrigued by the story of Bathsheba. She is often misunderstood and portrayed as an adulteress, but the reality is that she happened to be at the wrong place at the wrong time. Through scholarly research of Scripture and the culture of the time, we see that it was highly unlikely Bathsheba was guilty of anything at all. She was taking a bath outside, yes. However, when we learn that indoor plumbing wasn't a thing back then and it was normal for people to bathe outside—usually in a courtyard where there was at least some privacy—then we can conclude that Bathsheba was just doing what was normal for the time.

Bathsheba's suffering led her to bear fruit that grew while she was in the deepest valley of her life.

It's not uncommon to believe that the people who lived during biblical times were different than people today. In many ways, they were. However, God hasn't changed His recipe for creating people. They still had the same physical, emotional, and spiritual needs we have today. This means that Bathsheba likely felt a gamut of emotions as she experienced the consequences of sin—emotions we probably are all too familiar with as well. As we will see, Bathsheba's suffering led her to bear fruit that grew while she was in the deepest valley of her life, and her story shows us all how God restores and brings beauty from ashes every single time.

We've all experienced suffering, and let's face it: it's something we wouldn't wish on our worst enemy. One of my favorite verses from the Bible is John 16:33, which says, "In this world you will have trouble. But take heart! I have overcome the world." Jesus didn't say you might have trouble; He said you will have trouble. It doesn't get any clearer than that. Bathsheba is one woman from the Bible who experienced some hard stuff and lived to tell about it. In fact, she left a strong and lasting legacy even after surviving some of the most painful experiences.

When I was researching for my first book, *Heart Sisters*, I dug deeper into the story of Bathsheba and have been hooked ever since. While I had previously read this story, this time I studied it more thoroughly, and I immediately knew we would be friends if we lived at the same time. Bathsheba's my girl, a Heart Sister from another time, place, and, pretty much, world. I get her. Oh, how I get her, and I know you will too.

We first meet Bathsheba while she is bathing in 2 Samuel 11:2-4, "purifying herself from her monthly uncleanness" (v. 4). It was common for women to engage in ritual cleansing after menstruation, and as we've said, the bathtub was often located in an outdoor courtyard. These verses tell us that Bathsheba was very beautiful (v. 2) and that she was the wife of Uriah (v. 3), one of the most powerful warriors who was excruciatingly loyal to King David, and the daughter of Eliam (v. 3), a respected officer in David's regime. We also know that she was the granddaughter of Ahithophel (2 Samuel 23:34), who was one of King David's most trusted advisors. In other words, her lineage was solid. And because of the important roles the men in her life fulfilled for King David, she lived near his palace.

Up until this point in Scripture, the overall portrayal of David is as loyal, trusting, wise, respected. But the story of Bathsheba and David is where we catch a good glimpse of David's humanity and see that he was just as flawed and broken as the rest of us. Personally, I love this fact because it illustrates that we don't have to have it all figured out or be perfect for God to use us. However, David's sins affected many, many people—and certainly not for the better.

If we stay above reproach, we live below temptation.

Second Samuel 11:1 says, "In the spring, at the time when kings go off to war, David sent Joab out with the king's men and the whole Israelite army. They destroyed the Ammonites and besieged Rabbah. But David remained in Jerusalem." At first glance, this verse seems like one that simply provides a little background information and isn't terribly significant. Except . . . this verse is very significant. During this time in history, it was customary for kings to fight alongside their men; however, David wasn't with them. Instead, he stayed behind in Jerusalem, where he really wasn't supposed to be. How often does sin occur after someone is not where he or she is supposed to be? A spouse who is supposed to be working late ends up in a hotel room with a lover. A child who is supposed to be at a sleepover somehow ends up at that high school party. A friend who cancelled lunch with you and is supposed to be at home sick is having lunch with another friend. As I tell my children, put yourself in a situation where you might be tempted, and chances are you will be.

So since David wasn't where he was supposed to be and was, instead, at his palace, we discover that he took a little stroll on his roof and looked down to see a lovely woman taking a bath. Now, I never want to add anything to Scripture that isn't there, but I have to wonder. Did he not know who this woman was? With her impeccable pedigree from a line of notable men in David's close circle, did he not realize he was looking at Bathsheba? Nonetheless, he sent a messenger to find out her identity. Even after his messenger revealed Bathsheba's identity— daughter of Eliam and wife of Uriah—he sent for her. Even though she descended from notable men who had helped him and was married to one of his bravest warriors, he still pursued her. Even though he already had six other wives, he wanted her. David succumbed to his own lust and greed and used his power to get his way. If David had been where he was supposed to be in the first place, none of this would have happened. If we stay above reproach, we live below temptation.

As followers of Jesus, it's safe to assume we all desire to follow the narrow path. Ending up on the more-popular wide path leads to destruction, and we certainly don't want that. However, let's also just be real and recognize that most of us aren't really excited about having to work through the pain and suffering that gets us to the narrow path. Yet it's the narrow path that brings us life; and life is precisely what God wants for us all. Not just a content life here on this side of heaven, but also eternal life with Him. Bathsheba knew a thing or two about pain and suffering, and the story of her life will offer us motivation and hope to keep striving to reach—and stay on—the narrow, life-giving path. There are great rewards to the narrow path; and through trust, perseverance, and faith, we will eventually experience those rewards. That's some serious hope I think we can all get behind.

Turning to God

Prayerfully read and meditate on the following Scriptures:

Psalm 34:18
Psalm 46:1-3
Isaiah 41:10

Questions for Reflection or Discussion

1. Psalm 34:18 delivers a promise from God. What is that promise? How is this comforting to you? Do you believe this promise? Why or why not? Bathsheba was simply following what was customary at the time yet would soon find herself in a situation that isn't her choice and beyond her control. How does this verse comfort those who have been victimized by someone else's choices?

2. What evidence do you see in the world of many choosing to follow the wide path? What difference do you see between people who choose the narrow path and those who choose the wide path? What advantages and disadvantages are there to choosing each path? Which path bears more fruit and why?

3. Bathsheba descended from an impressive lineage of strong men who were well-respected and known; however, this did not protect her. How is this similar to those who experience trauma today? Does trauma discriminate? Why or why not?

4. Reflect on the statement "If we live above reproach, we live below temptation." How does this correlate with not being where we are supposed to be? Was David living above reproach? Why or why not? What about Bathsheba? How did David's choices affect her life?

5. Psalm 46:1-3 states that God is our refuge. When you think

of a refuge, what comes to mind? The Scripture says He is an ever-present help in times of trouble. Ever-present means He's always there. Have you felt God's presence in times of trouble? If so, when and how?

6. In Isaiah 41:10, we are told not to be afraid or dismayed because God is with us. We are promised His help and strength. In what ways does God offer us His help and strength?

7. How do you feel when you are around people who allow you to be your authentic self? How do you feel around those who make you want to hide your true self? Why is it important to God that we get real with Him? When we get real with God, does it help us to get real with others? Why or why not?

2

Understanding Your Pain and Suffering

It doesn't interest me to know where you live or how much money you have. I want to know if you can get up, after the night of grief and despair, weary and bruised to the bone, and do what needs to be done to feed the children.

—Oriah, "The Invitation"

J finally left," she said into the phone as I listened in shock on the other end. I knew my dear friend had been living in an abusive marriage for years, but I was still surprised to hear she had finally had enough. Although she did not know how everything would end, my friend's pain had reached the point she could no longer remain in her marriage. Her ex-husband's physical, verbal, and mental abuse had taken a toll on all aspects of her health. For years, I had watched her soul wither, and when the soul withers, we must do whatever it takes to bring it back to life. I privately prayed for her strength and courage to emerge while also praying for a miracle from God to restore her ex-husband and, in turn, their marriage. Either option would be beneficial for my friend.

It would have been far easier for her to stay in her marriage. If you've been through a divorce, then you know it can be financially and emotionally devastating. Yet after I realized her ex-husband was not going to stop the abuse, it became clear that divorce was necessary. Necessary for her mental health. Necessary for the health of her young daughter. And necessary for her soul. The early financial and emotional sacrifices were worth the freedom, security, and peace she now enjoys.

When the soul withers, we must do whatever it takes to bring it back to life.

If we're going to explore the concept of pain and suffering, it's helpful to understand some basic information on the science behind the pain we've experienced. But before we do, let's clear up a common misconception about trauma. Oftentimes we classify trauma as an intensely emotional experience, such as losing a loved one unexpectedly or witnessing violence or a severe accident. However, new research has discovered that well over half the population experiences some kind of traumatic event during their lives and every individual responds differently to their own trauma.[1] This explains why some people seem to bounce back after a painful event while others who may experience something similar have a more difficult time. Trauma encompasses more than witnessing accidents and combat; trauma also occurs when we've been horribly mistreated or deprived of something. When we see trauma through this lens, it's safe to say almost everyone has experienced trauma at some point in their lives. No one is immune to experiencing trauma, and it's far more common than we think.

While research on the biological response to trauma has been around for a while, it's not been as thorough as it has been since the turn of the twenty-first century. This relatively recent interest in trauma and its physical, psychological, and spiritual effect on survivors comes at a good time. Turn on the news at any given moment and you'll understand why there's a need to know more about how we are affected by trauma.

If we view our pain and suffering with an eternal perspective, our own brokenness can nourish our future souls and the souls of others.

When I first learned of the effect our mental health has on our physical health, I was fascinated. It's further evidence of how God created each of us to uniquely respond to our individual journey while, at the same time, knowing the story we would be able to tell. If we accept God's invitation of freely choosing Him, our stories will glorify Him. Choose Him, glorify Him. That's the deal. In fact, we are told we triumph over the enemy by Jesus and the words of our testimonies (Revelation 12:11). The second most powerful weapon for defeating our enemy is our story. Pretty powerful stuff.

But what if your story hasn't ever taken an unexpected turn? Hold tight, sister. It might someday. And since none of us gets out of here unscathed, I would say the chances are good you will walk through a valley at some point during your life. As my ninety-three-year-old grandmother always says, "Some people wear their fried eggs on the outside. Some people wear their fried eggs on the inside. But we all have them." In case you're confused, my Meemo uses the term *fried eggs* as a metaphor for brokenness. Maybe your fried eggs aren't as obvious as others', but you still have them because you're human. Those fried eggs of ours usually emerge as a result of our own pain and suffering—our own trauma. To be perfectly honest, I love fried eggs. They are an imperfect blob of goodness that ultimately gives us nourishment. If we view our pain and suffering with an eternal perspective, our own brokenness can nourish our future souls and the souls of others.

Both David and Bathsheba were certainly broken because they were human. But what trauma did they experience? In the previous chapter, we left off with Bathsheba bathing and catching the eye of King David. Let's read 2 Samuel 11:2-3a to review: "One evening David got up from his bed and walked around on the roof of the palace. From the roof he saw a woman bathing. The woman was very beautiful, and David sent someone to find out about her."

As soon as we realize that David wasn't where he was supposed to be and was watching a beautiful woman taking a bath, we can see where this is going. If you're guessing David succumbed to lust, you're right. Now let's see what happens when David's messenger returns: "The man said, 'She is Bathsheba, the daughter of Eliam and the wife of Uriah the Hittite.' Then David sent messengers to get her. She came to him, and he slept with her" (2 Samuel 11:3b-4a).

David knew full well the true identity of Bathsheba and yet still sent a messenger to summon her to the palace. Historically, when one was summoned by the king, there was not much choice but to follow his orders because the consequence for disobeying wasn't too pretty. So off Bathsheba went to the palace, where she found David, eagerly awaiting her arrival with plans of his own. David slept with Bathsheba, Bathsheba went home, and David was satisfied. End of story. Or so he thought.

Have you ever done something you thought you would get away with but then later realized you were going to be caught red-handed? My children love the story of the time my six-year-old self snatched a brand-spanking-new dress for a doll from my next-door neighbor's hands as she held it up for me to see. Turning swiftly on my heels, I dashed for her bedroom door, flew out the front door, sprinted to my house, and scurried up to my room where I hid the dress under my bed. I have no idea why I thought I would get away with such a thing, but all I knew was I wanted my doll to have that dress and I wanted it right then and there. I didn't care that it wasn't the right thing to do. I didn't care that my actions would hurt my best friend and neighbor. I didn't care that I was being selfish. I wanted the dress so I went for it—regardless of the cost.

On the one hand, while Scripture doesn't specifically state how David was feeling at this time, I can certainly hypothesize because, again, God didn't change His recipe for creating people. David was not off fighting with his men. He likely had more idle time than usual. He was bored and maybe even feeling a little guilty about not being where he was supposed to be. A new diversion might have piqued his interest and soothed his soul. Don't we all sometimes seek to soothe our souls with not-so-great stuff? Maybe it's overeating. Maybe it's alcohol. Maybe it's too much online shopping. Maybe it's video games. The point is, David might have seen Bathsheba as a fun diversion and a way to feel good—at least for a little while.

On the other hand, Scripture doesn't say how Bathsheba was feeling either, but as a woman, I can guess. I'm sure she was terrified because the punishment for adultery during this time was death by stoning. I'm also sure she felt powerless. Traumatized. Without a voice. Longing for the protection of her husband who was fighting a war. Alone.

And then she realized she was pregnant.

Realizing he had backed himself into a corner, David devised a plan he thought would get him out of the whole thing. In 2 Samuel 11:6-13, he summoned Bathsheba's husband, Uriah, back to the palace and asked him a few questions about the war. David then told Uriah to go home and relax, hoping Uriah might sleep with Bathsheba. Then David could pass the child in Bathsheba's womb off as Uriah's, and he'd be off scot-free. But Uriah refused to do so. Instead, like the servants, he slept on a mat at the entrance of the palace because he was a man of integrity and didn't think it would be respectable to sleep with his wife while his men were fighting a battle.

The next day, David upped his game and prepared a large feast with a lot of wine. Translation? He planned to get Uriah really drunk so maybe he would go home on the second night. You may not be shocked to learn Uriah stayed right on his little mat at the palace entrance. But as we are about to see, David's sin was taking him even deeper than he ever wanted to go, which is so often the case with sin.

Do you know the quote about the best-laid plans? The best-laid plans of mice and men often go awry.[2] David's plans went terribly awry when Uriah, a man of honor and integrity, refused to go home to his wife the entire time he was visiting the palace. David's plan was thwarted, his panic intensified, and what happened next was even worse: after Uriah returned to battle, David ordered him to the front lines, where he was killed.

So now Bathsheba had been forced to commit adultery, was pregnant with an illegitimate child, and her husband was dead. I'd say Bathsheba was experiencing some trauma, wouldn't you?

Sadly, the story doesn't end there. There's more trauma to come. But before we explore the next part of the story, let's talk a little bit about what happens to your physical body when you experience trauma. And remember, trauma is any distressing or painful event, which means trauma is far more common than usually believed.

Between 1995 and 1997, the Centers for Disease Control and Prevention (CDC) and Kaiser Permanente conducted a study to determine what happens to our health and overall well-being when we experience childhood trauma.[3] What was revealed was perhaps not shocking in that it proved there is indeed a strong correlation between the pain and suffering we experience and our physical health as we go through life. Researchers discovered that high doses of trauma affect brain development, the immune system, the hormonal system, and even how DNA is interpreted. For many of us, this isn't a huge shock as we know God created us to be physical, spiritual, and mental beings. When one of these areas is off, the other two are affected.

The brain is a vast and complex organ including an area called the nucleus accumbens. This area is the pleasure and reward center and plays a significant role in addiction. Those who have experienced high levels of trauma have a compromised nucleus accumbens, thus leading to a higher chance of alcohol use by the age of fourteen and illicit drug use by the age of fifteen. Trauma exposure also inhibits the prefrontal cortex, the part of the brain responsible for impulse control and higher-level thinking—both critical areas for learning. For this reason, many children who have experienced trauma are incorrectly labeled as having attention deficit disorder with hyperactivity (ADHD) and tend to engage in riskier behavior as they mature.

Lastly, the amygdala, the part of the brain responsible for keeping us safe in the event a wild coyote should chase us across a meadow, is affected by trauma as well. God created us with an amygdala so we would be able to flee from danger without even having to think about it. Coined the "fight or flight response," this is a great thing if you are indeed being chased by a wild animal; however, the problem occurs when you're not. Those who have experienced trauma can downshift into the fight-or-flight response any time they are exposed to even the smallest amount of stress because they've been conditioned to simply survive for so much of their lives.

I don't know about you, but learning this information is a game-changer for me as a former educator, mother, and counselor-in-training. Trauma has the power to change our physical, emotional, and spiritual selves.

There were other interesting facts in this study. For example, 74.8 percent of the participants were Caucasian. In addition, 35.9 percent had some college experience while 39.3 percent had college or advanced graduate degrees. Perhaps not surprising, 60 percent of the population reported experiencing at least one adverse childhood experience (ACE) by their sixteenth birthday. I tell you this so you understand that the sorts of traumas we've discussed here are not endemic to one population or another, and we should not rush to assumptions about one demographic or another. Trauma is something that affects all of us.

When we keep our pain in the dark, we give the enemy the reins; but when we surrender our pain to the light, we give the reins to God.

Aren't you just so excited to invite me to your next dinner party? I know I'm a ball of fun right about now. But we have to talk about some of this hard stuff, the stuff no one really wants to talk about, because it's so important to bring our pain and suffering into the light. When we keep our suffering in the dark, the enemy is able to do his best work. We fill in details we don't know or understand with false assumptions not based on truth. We feel accused by the accuser. We doubt God, just like the serpent taught Eve to do in the garden. When we keep our pain in the dark, we give the enemy the reins; but when we surrender our pain to the light, we give the reins to God. I know which one I want to pick.

The light is where the real healing begins. God is the light, so when we pull our pain from the darkness into the light, we are placing it right in the palms of the hands of a loving Father whose heart is even more broken over your heartbreak than you are. The enemy is no longer able to influence our faulty thinking because it's in God's hands, and the enemy can't ever hold a candle to God. Oh, the enemy will try to take back the reins. But when we start working through the healing process, we are more able to recognize when he's trying to do just that and can readily give the control back to God.

How do we bring our pain to the light? We'll dive more into this in Part Two; however, the first step you can take today is to pray and surrender it to God. Healing is a process; so while some immediately feel set free from their pain, not everyone does. However, the first step of healing is to recognize you cannot carry your burdens alone anymore. I love the words of Matthew 11:28-30: "Come to me, all you who are weary and burdened, and I will give you rest. Take my yoke upon you and learn from me, for I am gentle and humble in heart, and you will find rest for your souls. For my yoke is easy and my burden is light." Oftentimes I will read scripture in one version and then compare it to another. I love how *The Message* summarizes these verses: "Are you tired? Worn out? Burned out on religion? Come to me. Get away with me and you'll recover your life. I'll show you how to take a real rest. Walk with me and work with me; watch how I do it. Learn the unforced rhythms of grace. I won't lay anything heavy or ill-fitting on you. Keep company with me and you'll learn to live freely and lightly." Living freely and lightly sounds wonderful, doesn't it?

All of our pain and suffering, which is our trauma, affects our lives. Healing this trauma certainly isn't easy; however, the reward for having the courage to start the process of healing from your trauma has the power to change the complete trajectory of your family line. As we'll see, David and Bathsheba's certainly did. Regardless of your pain and suffering, let me offer us all a nice, heaping platter of hope: you can absolutely be set free from the pain you've endured in the past. You can absolutely heal from any trauma you have endured. And you can absolutely live in peace, hope, and contentment—regardless of what's in your rearview mirror.

As we conclude this chapter, I want to share a passage of scripture that often offers me such hope.

But now, God's Message,
>   the God who made you in the first place, Jacob,
>   the One who got you started, Israel:
> "Don't be afraid, I've redeemed you.
>   I've called your name. You're mine.
> When you're in over your head, I'll be there with you.
>   When you're in rough waters, you will not go
>   down.
> When you're between a rock and a hard place,
>   it won't be a dead end—
> Because I am God, your personal God,
>   The Holy of Israel, your Savior.
> I paid a huge price for you:
>   all of Egypt, with rich Cush and Seba thrown in!
> That's how much you mean to me!
>   That's how much I love you!
> I'd sell off the whole world to get you back,
>   trade the creation just for you."
>   (Isaiah 43:1-4 MSG)

You are His. You. Yes, you. You've been redeemed. You've been called by name. When you feel like you're in over your head, God is there. You won't drown when you're in rough waters. You won't be stuck. You were bought for a huge price, and your worth to God is immeasurable. In fact, you mean so much to God that He would sell off the whole world to get you back.

That's an unfathomable love, friend, and it's true.

Turning to God

Prayerfully read and meditate on the following Scriptures:

Exodus 15:26
Psalm 103:2-3
Jeremiah 31:3-4
1 Peter 2:24

Questions for Reflection or Discussion

1. What are some of your reactions to the information about trauma in this chapter? Was there anything that surprised you? Why or why not?

2. Exodus 15:26 says, "For I am the LORD, who heals you." How have you allowed God to heal you? What areas of your heart are still in need of healing? Take a moment to take this first step of the healing journey by releasing it to God in prayer.

3. Is there specific pain you are still keeping in the dark? What could you do to bring that pain to the light? List steps and consider following up those steps with action. How can you support others who are healing as well?

4. What gives you hope? Has hope ever sustained you through a rough valley? Reflect for a moment on what it would be like to live without hope. What does that look like? Sound like? Feel like? Now reflect on what it's like to live with hope. What does that look like? Sound like? Feel like? Compare the two and make a choice of how you want to live.

5. First Peter 2:24 says that we are healed by Christ's wounds. What does this mean? Why is this important to understand in our healing journey?

6. Psalm 103:2-3 says, "Praise the LORD, my soul, and forget not

all his benefits—who forgives all your sins and heals all your diseases." What are the benefits we are not supposed to forget? Even in the midst of our suffering, we are to praise God, but sometimes this is just plain hard.

7. Scripture does not specifically say how Bathsheba was feeling after being forced to have sex with David, becoming pregnant, then enduring the murder of her husband. However, since God didn't change the recipe for people, how do you think she felt? Name three emotions she was likely feeling. Do you know any Scripture references that could offer comfort to someone feeling like this?

8. After becoming pregnant by David and the death of her husband, Bathsheba's life takes a very unexpected turn. Read Jeremiah 31:3-4. What three promises does God make in these verses? How can this offer comfort when life takes an unexpected turn?

3

Choosing Your Response

You may kill me with your hatefulness,
But still, like air, I'll rise.
                    —Maya Angelou, "Still I Rise"

One of my friends has an adage that goes something like this: "You can get glad in the same pants you got sad (or mad) in!" If we can sift through the grammatical errors of this statement and look at the message, we can decipher the main idea: your own happiness or sadness depends on the attitude you choose. Now, this doesn't mean we shouldn't ever be sad. God created us to experience emotions, and personally I'm a big fan of sitting in your sadness for a bit because if we don't, we can add to our own trauma. In chapter eight, we will further explore how failure to process our grief and instead rush the healing journey will hurt us in the long run.

Choosing how we react will affect what we attract. Our perspective controls the directive.

However, sitting in our sadness for too long can lead to feeling sorry for ourselves and, in turn, can cause us to become mopey and miserable.

In the beloved book *Winnie-the-Pooh*, there are two characters who are polar opposites of each other: Tigger, an energetic, joy-filled tiger, and Eeyore, a downcast, woe-is-me donkey. We don't have to always be Tigger, but we certainly don't want to always be Eeyore, right? Choosing how we react will affect what we attract. In other words, if we are mopey and sad all the time, we'll probably see the world through a mopey and sad lens. If we are content and joy-filled, then we'll see a world of contentment and joy. Our perspective controls the directive.

Bathsheba didn't ask for David to summon her to the palace. She just happened to be taking a bath—a normal custom for women of this time to follow after menstruation. Since she had to bathe outside, there wasn't much privacy; however, most people would not be able to see her. King David had a vantage point because his palace included a high rooftop he could walk upon. Looking down, he could easily see into what was very likely the courtyard in which Bathsheba was bathing. Bathsheba was an innocent woman not breaking any rules. Another person's choice to sin caused her great heartache and sadness.

After Bathsheba's husband, Uriah, was killed following King David's order to move him to the front line, she mourned his loss. Once the period of mourning was complete, David summoned her to his palace again; but this time instead of forcing her to sleep with him, David married her. Sure, the whole thing was a disaster. Sure, David sinned like crazy. And sure, both David and Bathsheba most certainly experienced emotional trauma. But the problem had been taken care of, and now Bathsheba could birth their child in peace without the accusation of adultery. Whew.

Except...not so much. David failed to consider one very important piece of this hot-mess of a puzzle: you can't hide from God. God was very aware of what his anointed king had done, and He certainly wasn't going to let David off the hook. In 2 Samuel 12, Nathan, a court prophet during David's reign, was sent by God to discuss David's sin. Cleverly,

Nathan presented David's situation as a parable, a story of two different people in which he hoped David would judge. His story went like this:

> There were two men in a certain town, one rich and the other poor. The rich man had a very large number of sheep and cattle, but the poor man had nothing except one little ewe lamb he had bought. He raised it, and it grew up with him and his children. It shared his food, drank from his cup and even slept in his arms. It was like a daughter to him.
>
> Now a traveler came to the rich man, but the rich man refrained from taking one of his own sheep or cattle to prepare a meal for the traveler who had come to him. Instead, he took the ewe lamb that belonged to the poor man and prepared it for the one who had come to him. (2 Samuel 12:1-4)

Can you tell which man is David and which is Uriah? Let's see how David reacted:

> David burned with anger against the man and said to Nathan, "As surely as the LORD lives, the man who did this must die! He must pay for that lamb four times over, because he did such a thing and had no pity." (2 Samuel 12:5-6)

Ouch. Because then Nathan told David he was actually the greedy, rich man and God wasn't too pleased with him. After David heard this, he was humbled and admitted he'd sinned against the Lord. But that didn't excuse him from God's discipline. Sadly, 2 Samuel 12:13-14 explains the consequence David will face. Nathan said, "The LORD has taken away your sin. You are not going to die. But because by doing this you have shown utter contempt for the LORD, the son born to you will die."

Whoa. God wasn't messing around here, was He?

A few days ago, one of my children made a not-so-great choice. We disciplined him, and through his flood of tears he said he was concerned we wouldn't forgive him. Besides the fact this devastated my mama heart because I thought our children understood there is nothing they could ever do to prohibit our forgiveness, I explained the purpose of discipline. We discipline our children because we love them too much not discipline them.

The same is true of God. Because there is never any condemnation in Christ (Romans 8:1), we know we can never be condemned by God for our sins. Punishment is condemnation while discipline is correction—the kind of correction a loving parent would offer their child. Discipline is how we encourage our children to choose obedience rather than rebellion because we can see the big picture. The same is true of God; He has an eternal perspective we can't see. He disciplines us so we can stop rebelling and instead choose to obey.

But what about Bathsheba? you may be thinking. *She doesn't deserve discipline. She didn't do anything wrong!* And you are absolutely correct. Sometimes other people suffer the consequences of another person's sin because fairness is not always part of the deal on this side of heaven. I'm reminded of when my children say, "It's just not fair!" Oftentimes it's not, and I understand. And I'm guessing you also know that life isn't always fair, right? However, God sees those who suffer at the hands of someone else. *The Message* wording of 1 Peter 2:18-19 sheds some light for us:

> You who are servants, be good servants to your
> masters—not just to good masters, but also to bad
> ones. What counts is that you put up with it for God's

sake when you're treated badly for no good reason. There's no particular virtue in accepting punishment that you well deserve. But if you're treated badly for good behavior and continue in spite of it to be a good servant, that is what counts with God.

We are all servants of God. When we are mistreated despite our good behavior and lack of sin, what counts most is that we continue with our good behavior despite the poor treatment. If you've ever been in this situation, you know how horribly difficult this is to do. There are two kinds of grace: behavior grace and forgiveness grace. Choosing to rise above and keep our eyes focused on God while simultaneously behaving in a way that pleases Him is behavior grace. God wants our behavior grace because doing what's right is easy when you're being treated kindly. It's when we aren't being treated kindly that we show God the stuff we're made of.

Bathsheba could choose to become a survivor of her circumstances or a victim of her vulnerabilities.

So now, because of David's lust and greed, Bathsheba has lost her husband. She's married to the man who caused the whole mess and pregnancy. And the discipline for David's actions is the life of the child growing in her womb. I just have to guess how Bathsheba must be feeling since Scripture doesn't spell it out for us. I'm certain she was still grieving the loss of her husband, and when we're grieving, our emotions can go from zero to sixty in three seconds. Yet she still had a choice as to how she would react. Bathsheba could choose to become a survivor of her circumstances or a victim of her vulnerabilities. As we will soon discover, Bathsheba chose to be a survivor, and that choice affected us all. Aren't you excited to hear how this all ends? I don't ever tire of hearing Bathsheba's story, and I think you'll be hooked by the end of this book too.

When the inevitable valleys of life appear in our journey, we can choose to become either a victim or a survivor. A victim is someone who experiences something difficult and allows it to define them from that point forward. Their hardship becomes an excuse for an attitude of defeat and self-pity. Victims have an external locus of control, meaning it doesn't matter what they say or do; the world will always work against them. In their minds, they have no control over their lives; life happens to them.

Like trauma, victim mentality can also have a detrimental effect on our physical health. Since victims typically see the world through a lens that says the world is against them and they're never safe, they tend to adapt to a negative way of thinking. Negative thinking often leads to an increase in the amount of time spent in "fight or flight" mode. This can lead to the production of excess cortisol and adrenaline, which, in turn, leads to anxiety, adrenal fatigue, and sleep interruption. In addition, if someone already struggles with an illness or disease, victim mentality will inhibit and slow down the healing process.

However, you could choose to pursue healing and become a survivor of your circumstances, seeking help as necessary. Survivors have learned the skill of resilience—in other words, the ability to "bounce back" after the setbacks of life occur. While resilience is usually instilled through at least one loving and supportive caregiver during childhood, it can also be developed at any point during our lives—often with the help of a counselor or other equipped professional. Resilience allows a survivor to accept and understand what happened to them and use it to build their own strength while also eventually helping others with the same struggle. Survivors are resilient, reflective, and thoughtfully responsive. They make the choice not to live as a victim and, instead, choose to become better, not bitter.

Bathsheba had a choice too. She could have become a victim, embittered by the raw deal she had been dealt. She could have lived under the umbrella of shame and retreated from society. She could have chosen to perseverate on the great injustices she suffered even though she was blameless and had done nothing wrong. She could have constantly felt unsafe, succumbing to a life of fear. However, this isn't how Bathsheba chose to react. In the next chapter we'll see proof that Bathsheba became a survivor, not a victim. This one choice still affects all of us to this very day.

To end this chapter, let's look at what Scripture has to say about becoming a victim or a survivor. Romans 8:35-39 says this:

> Who shall separate us from the love of Christ? Shall trouble or hardship or persecution or famine or nakedness or danger or sword? As it is written:
>
> "For your sake we face death all day long;
>   we are considered as sheep to be slaughtered."
>
> No, in all these things we are more than conquerors through him who loved us. For I am convinced that neither death nor life, neither angels nor demons, neither the present nor the future, nor any powers, neither height nor depth, nor anything else in all creation, will be able to separate us from the love of God that is in Christ Jesus our Lord.

Nothing can separate us from Jesus, friends. Absolutely nothing. No pain or suffering. No persecution. No hardship. Nada. It's true that, as Christians, we're open to the skepticism and criticism of others, and sometimes it can feel like we're sheep about to be slaughtered. But the thing is, we're not because we are more than conquerors. Victims are not conquerors. They're negative and wallow in self-pity.

Victims choose to stay in their pain with blame while survivors choose to go use their pain for good.

Survivors are more than conquerors. They look their adversity in the eye and, whether they suffer because of their own choices or because of someone else's, say "Nope, not today." This doesn't mean there aren't tears and lamentations of "Why me?" It just means they won't stay there forever. Victims choose to stay in their pain with blame while survivors choose to go use their pain for good.

You want to know what's really great? If you are reading this and you suspect you might be operating with a victim mentality, guess what? You can change that. When we recognize that we are not powerless and can choose how we respond, our first response can be the relinquishment of our victim perspective. Recognizing we think this way is the first step to becoming a survivor. Processing our pain with a good counselor who understands the benefit of being a survivor instead of a victim is invaluable. After a session with my counselor, I'm always amazed by how faulty my own perspective and thinking can be. Sometimes sharing our hearts with someone who is trained to listen can allow us to identify our thinking errors and kick them to the curb.

Taking responsibility for your healing is the next step following your decision to no longer be a victim. It takes far more courage to be survivor, and I am confident you have it in you, sister.

Turning to God

Prayerfully read and meditate on the following Scriptures:

2 Corinthians 1:3-4
Hebrews 12:7-13
James 1:12

Questions for Reflection or Discussion

1. What do you think of when you hear the word *victim*? Compare victims and survivors. How are they alike? How are they different?

2. Hebrews 12:7-13 is powerful. Read through these verses again. What does it mean to endure hardship as discipline? How can we reconcile a loving God with the hardship we face in this world? Why does God allow hardship, and how can He use it for our good? What does "discipline" eventually produce according to verses 10-11?

3. Revelation 12:11 says that we will overcome sin by Jesus and the words of our testimonies. Reread 2 Corinthians 1:3-4. How is this verse similar? What is one reason God comforts us?

4. James talks quite a bit about suffering. Read James 1:12. In this verse, the word *blessed* means someone who possesses courageous determination regardless of their circumstances. How is this related to being a survivor? What does this have to do with resilience? Why is resilience important, and how do you think we can build up resilience?

5. Reflect for a moment on Bathsheba's story up to this point. How do you think she was feeling? How do you think she will choose to react, and why?

6. How do you think David will react after being confronted with his sin by Nathan? Do you think he will choose to act differently as a result of his sin? Why or why not? If you are familiar with the story and know how David reacts, compare his reaction to how many react to the same offense today. How are they different? Which reaction is what God desires and why?

~ 4 ~

Turning Away from Shame

Suffering, failure, loneliness, sorrow, discouragement, and death will be part of your journey, but the Kingdom of God will conquer all these horrors. No evil can resist grace forever.

—Brennan Manning

Who hasn't heard the phrase "Shame on you!" at some point during their lives? These words make me cringe because if we truly knew the long-term negative effect of shame, we would never speak this over anyone, even our worst enemies. Shame holds us captive but releases our perception of reality. This misconception leaves us vulnerable to believing lies—lies that are never, ever from God and always from the enemy.

I know shame well, friend. During the first twenty-seven years of my life, I lived for me. I was all about my own needs, desires, beliefs, and thoughts. When you live for yourself, you oftentimes make choices that later lead to feelings of shame, and I sure did. I'm not proud of some of the decisions I made. I'm guessing you might know a thing or two about that kind of shame as well. Suffering from the ill effects of shame is far more common than we often initially believe because shame doesn't discriminate. Everyone experiences shame at some point, but it's how we react that determines whether or not we'll sink into a shame storm or rise above it.

Dr. Brene Brown accidentally stumbled upon the opportunity to research shame and has contributed greatly to our understanding of the shame cycle. Dr. Brown describes shame as "an intensely painful feeling or experience of believing that we are flawed and therefore unworthy of love and belonging."[1] Shame tells us we are unlovable. It says we are not worthy. We are less than. We are not liked. We are flawed. Shame makes us believe we are defined by our sin or what was done to us. Shame is, of course, a liar. Yet it's often so difficult to identify those lies when we're up to our necks in the tight grip of shame that refuses to budge.

We don't have to look any further than the second chapter in the Book of Genesis to find the first mention of the word *shame*. Genesis 2:25 says that "Adam and his wife were both naked, and they felt no shame." We were initially created to never feel any shame. Ever. Can you imagine living a life where shame simply didn't exist? Adam and Eve were naked, yet Eve never worried about how her body looked to Adam, and vice versa. Shame simply wasn't a thing.

Yet as we read the next chapter of Genesis, we are introduced to the serpent. The serpent represents Satan himself, determined to tempt Eve by raising doubt and uncertainty. Immediately after Adam and Eve were deceived and disobeyed God by eating the fruit from the forbidden tree, they realized they were naked and sewed fig leaves together to hide their bodies. Next, they heard God coming and hid from Him because they were ashamed of their nakedness. Shame was the first negative emotion to enter the scene after Adam and Eve ate the fruit from the tree of the knowledge of good and evil. Make no bones about it, shame is directly from the enemy.

If we find ourselves wanting to hide something, that's shame. As we discussed in the previous chapter, when we keep our pain and suffering in the dark, hidden in shame, the enemy can do the most destruction.

He's better able to feed us lies and distort our thinking so he can sit back and watch us attack ourselves, because shame is the enemy's specialty. It makes his goal of our destruction very attainable because he loves it when we hide our pain and mask our suffering.

Wearing masks is a form of hiding that leads to the inability to be authentic in relationships. In my book *Heart Sisters* I talk about "pretty front porch friends." These friends are the ones who seem to have it all figured out—at least, that's how it appears. Their "front porch" is always beautiful and put together; however, you'll never be invited into their messy living room because they're too ashamed you'll uncover the truth. They're petrified you will realize they don't actually have life all figured out. And because the enemy loves when we keep our shame hidden, he likes those masks to stay firmly in place. When we hide our authentic selves from others, we create a barrier that blocks the growth of healthy relationships. The problem with this? We heal from our pain through authentic and healthy relationships. We'll unpack this further in chapter ten, but the bottom line is this: shame negatively influences our relationships. Pretty much all of them. If we trace many of our negative emotions back to the root, we often will find shame.

While talking about shame to a friend one day, she asked, "Isn't shame sometimes a good thing?" She went on to explain that it's shame that convicts us to change behavior we need to change or turn away from sin. However, my friend was actually referring to guilt. Yes, believe it or not, guilt can be a positive emotion if it does indeed encourage us to turn away from sin or change destructive behavior. Guilt tells us we did something wrong and need to make it right, while shame tells us we are a terrible person and aren't worthy of anyone's love or respect.

I'm notorious for forgetting to look under my cart when I'm checking out at the grocery store. Even with those automated reminders. Too much on my plate and already thinking about what I must do next, I hit that forward button and wrap it all up. I've got stuff to do. I feel like you might get this. Except the other day, I arrived at the trunk of my car to realize I had a case of water in the bottom of my cart and had not paid for it. Did I mention I was already ten minutes late for picking up my daughter? So I threw the water in my trunk and proceeded to race across town.

Shame takes healthy guilt and allows it to penetrate the walls of our souls until they crumble into a heaping mess.

Later as I was unpacking my groceries, the guilt emerged. I didn't pay for that water. If you take something from a store without paying for it, that's stealing. The more I thought about it, the more I realized I needed to go back to the store and pay for the water. I did, and I have to say that the clerk thought I was completely nuts. But I don't care. Guilt prodded me to do the right thing in this situation, and I left the store feeling better. I am a person in need of grace who made a mistake. The end.

So while guilt can be positive and convict us to move toward positive behavior and change, shame is on the other end of the spectrum. Let's say my reaction to the case of water situation was, "I am a terrible, awful person. I am a thief. No one should ever be friends with me. I am not worthy of love of any kind." There you go—shame, shame, shame. Shame takes healthy guilt and allows it to penetrate the walls of our souls until they crumble into a heaping mess. In other words, we allow shame to label us and tell us who we are because we've believed lies that do not originate in any way, shape, or form from God. Shame is toxic to the heart, mind, and soul of every sufferer.

Even worse, it's not uncommon for shame to lead to other choices that could invoke even more shame. Oftentimes to remedy our resultant anxiety and depression, we attempt to medicate ourselves with too much alcohol, too much shopping, too much eating, or too much anything. All of this "too much" leads us to feel even more ashamed, and we just keep falling deeper and deeper down the shame rabbit hole.

The Bible doesn't say anything about Bathsheba feeling shame, but as a woman I can make a pretty good guess that she did. There is no doubt in my mind that Bathsheba felt some shame, friend. When we look at the role of women during this time period, they weren't encouraged to speak their minds or clarify truth—especially when the perpetrator was none other than King David himself.

Can you imagine if the David and Bathsheba story happened today? There would be headlines that might or might not be true. Very likely, Bathsheba would be portrayed as a beguiling seductress, determined to gain a more powerful husband and accrue more wealth. How clever of her to get pregnant too—financial support forever! While this seems like a silly thought, we have to remember that God didn't change His recipe for creating people. There may not have been social media or online news sources, but word traveled fast by mouth then too. And you better believe there was talk about David and Bathsheba. In fact, that talk still plagues Bathsheba today, as she is oftentimes still portrayed as the conniving adulteress.

While we can only assume Bathsheba experienced feelings of shame, we see evidence of David's shame when he panicked after learning Bathsheba was pregnant. Can you imagine his first thought? "Oh, man, I'm in big trouble; I have to do something to cover this up" was probably right up there. In 2 Samuel 11:6, David immediately sent for Uriah, indicating he had already concocted a plan to hide his sin and move on. When we want to hide ourselves or something we've done, then we know it's steeped in shame. David's shame resulting from his sin led to even more shame following the success of his plot to cause Uriah's death. Shame leads to more shame, and the cycle continues until we have the courage to break it.

One of my friends is the survivor of a horrific sexual assault that happened while she was in college years ago. She fought a brutal battle with shame in the years following, and it affected all areas of her life. She blamed herself because she thought maybe she wore something that encouraged the perpetrator to think she wanted something she didn't. She thought she should be "over it" after a year or two, so she felt shame for still hurting. She felt horrible that she had not tried to help other victims of sexual assault. She saw herself as "damaged goods," unable to be in a healthy sexual relationship or ever trust a romantic partner. The shame she felt told her lies that inhibited her healing for years.

It wasn't until she sought help from a compassionate counselor that she was able to name what she was feeling. When we identify our shame, we take the first step of kicking it to the curb. My friend was able to reconcile the fact that she was not guilty of a single thing, and while she was a victim of sexual assault, she no longer needed to live as a victim. We choose how we respond, and she changed her response by declaring her commitment to healing. We often heal through relationships, and my friend's relationship with her counselor literally changed the entire trajectory of her life.

Coined by Dr. Brown, the term *shame resilience* means we can work through our impending shame by identifying it, choosing how to respond, and expressing more compassion and love for others as a result of our experience. Brown further notes that if you want to kill shame dead in its tracks, share your story with an empathetic listener, which is exactly what my friend did when she told her counselor of her sexual assault and her shame-related responses.[2] She killed shame. Shame can't survive when we share our stories with someone who listens with compassion. Remember: the enemy doesn't want us to kill shame because then we will no longer be under his spell. It takes courage to claim the Word of God, but when we do, the enemy shrinks back and cowers. I don't know about you, but I love the thought of the enemy cowering under my Almighty God who protects me, loves me, and would do anything for my freedom.

Releasing our shame is a process, one that requires commitment and courage. If you struggle with toxic shame, I pray this chapter has allowed you to recognize why it is important to release it and embrace who God created you to be. The truth is, you are loved with an everlasting love. You are forgiven as far as the east is from the west. You are fearfully and wonderfully made. You are His masterpiece. You will never be abandoned nor forsaken. You are His chosen daughter.

Now walk in that truth, sister. He has been waiting for you to do just that.

Turning to God

Prayerfully read and meditate on the following Scriptures:

2 Corinthians 3:17
Galatians 5:1
Philippians 1:6

Questions for Reflection or Discussion

1. Reread Philippians 1:6. How can living under shame keep you from doing the good works God has planned for you to do?
2. What advice would you give Bathsheba if she told you she was struggling with shame? If you are struggling with shame, what is keeping you from following this advice?
3. Second Corinthians 3:17 says that "where the Spirit of the Lord is, there is freedom." The Holy Spirit, as part of the Holy Trinity, comes to dwell in us when we accept Christ as our Savior, which means that we have an advocate living in us who has defeated sin and death. If your shame is a result of your own past sin, there is freedom. If your shame is a result of a part of you that has died after experiencing trauma through no fault of your own, there is freedom. Why do you think freedom helps us overcome shame?
4. Galatians 5:1 encourages us to "stand firm, then, and do not let yourselves be burdened again by a yoke of slavery." Who or what do we need to stand firm against? How can we become slaves to our own shame? How do we become victors over our shame?
5. Can you think of times when guilt has actually been a positive

force in your life? Did it encourage you to change your behavior or choices? When does guilt become unhealthy?

6. Shame makes us vulnerable to believe the lies from the one who only wants to steal, kill, and destroy (John 10:10). What lies do you think Bathsheba might have believed?

❧ 5 ❧

Turning Away from Anger

Did I offer peace today? Did I bring a smile to someone's face? Did I say words of healing? Did I let go of my anger and resentment? Did I forgive? Did I love? These are the real questions.

I must trust that the little bit of love that I sow now will bear many fruits, here in this world and the life to come.

—Henri Nouwen,
"Sabbatical Journey"

It had been a very, very long day. I mean, the kind of day where the clock reads seven o'clock in the morning but it feels like it should already be bedtime. There were three children under the age of four running through my house, the dog was missing, and I forgot we were supposed to be at a doctor's appointment by 8:30. With three small children, having only an hour to get everyone fed, clothed, and in car seats was not enough time. Never mind if I wanted to look somewhat presentable. Ever had those moments when you beg Jesus to come down and save you right in that very moment so you can get out of whatever it is you have to do? Well, that was one of those moments for me.

Needless to say, I lost my stuff that morning. Big time. I yelled. I released dramatic sighs. I lamented about how I needed help. After my tantrum, as the tears spilled from my eyes, all I could think of was how much I was failing as a mom. My anger boiled over, and afterward I was overcome with intense shame. Thoughts like "Other moms seem to do this much better than me" and "I'm going to do long-term damage to my children because of my anger" began to eat away at me until I started to believe they were true.

Here's the thing: some of it was true. In the last chapter we talked about how guilt can convict us to make positive changes in our behavior. While I certainly did allow my thoughts to become shameful by believing other moms were doing better than I was, it's true that my own anger issues could have a negative effect on my children. This conviction could easily go to a place of shame if I started to believe I was just a bad mother and person in general. Instead, after I emerged from my shame storm, I used this guilt to begin working on my struggle with anger.

Working through our anger is another good choice we can make for our physical health. Researchers recently discovered our automatic responses to anger can lead to headaches, anxiety and depression, digestive issues, insomnia, heart attack, and skin irritations.[1] We simply can't afford to leave our anger unchecked.

Shame and anger are contagious, but not if we catch them before they spread.

The thing about anger is *it's often a response to shame*. Interestingly enough, shame is the only emotion that can attach to other emotions. For this reason, we can feel anger while also feeling shame. This anger/shame combo pack can cause us to lash out at others, lash out at ourselves, or avoid conflict with people altogether. Obviously, none of these is a healthy response, and all three cause a buildup that will eventually boil over or boil in.

When we lash out at others, we oftentimes direct our anger toward those we love the most. It's a horrible feeling, isn't it? Nothing can send me down the shame spiral faster than throwing a tantrum with my family as the victims. Eventually, the recipients of our anger begin to deal with their own shame. I certainly don't want to be the source of shame for anyone, and guess what? Giving shame away can cause us to feel even deeper shame if we don't build up our own shame resiliency. Shame and anger are contagious, but not if we catch them before they spread.

We can also direct our anger inward toward ourselves. When we fail to offer ourselves grace, we're set up for a lifetime of disappointment because the thing is, we are all human beings who can be disabled by the flesh. We are going to make mistakes. We are going to fall short— and fall short often. We are going to say things we shouldn't say and do things we shouldn't do. But Jesus came so we don't have to bear what we should rightfully receive as a consequence. Grace and mercy, the two best gifts from God, were born the second Jesus died on the cross; and when we don't extend that grace and mercy to ourselves, we aren't accepting His gift.

Anger of any kind left to simmer will eventually boil over, burning ourselves the most.

Scripture has a lot to say about anger and rage too. Ecclesiastes 7:9 tells us that anger resides in the laps of fools. Colossians 3:8 says we must rid ourselves of all anger, rage, malice, and filthy language. Proverbs 22:24 flat-out warns us to avoid friendship with someone who is easily angered and hot-tempered. And Proverbs 29:11 says that fools vent their rage but the wise bring calm in the end. I think it's safe to say that God understands how anger can rip apart relationships—with others and with ourselves.

Yet there were times in the New Testament when Jesus became angry. For example, He overturned tables because money-changers were selling goods in the temple. Isn't this anger? It sure is. But it's righteous anger. Righteous anger and the kind of anger God warns us of throughout Scripture are very, very different. Righteous anger is anger directed at sin. We absolutely can and should be angry about human trafficking. We absolutely can and should be angry about abuse. We absolutely can and should be angry about racism or discrimination. Righteous anger and sin anger are two very different animals. However, righteous anger can become sin anger if we allow it to fester too long. Anger of any kind left to simmer will eventually boil over, burning ourselves the most.

Now let me be clear about something: it's perfectly normal to feel angry when we have been wronged. Many have experienced great injustice and are survivors of terrible stuff. If that is you, I am so sorry. Jesus is absolutely righteously enraged by your suffering. It's actually important for you to feel that anger and grieve, as we will discuss in more detail in chapter eight.

God will always find a way to reconstruct something good when deconstruction threatens to destroy.

We don't know if Bathsheba struggled with anger, but considering that she had been forced to have sex with the king, her husband was killed, and she lost her first child all because of David's sin, I'm going to go out on a limb here and say she probably did. She most certainly was entitled to feel righteous anger because we know God was angry with David. If God is angry, you can be assured it's righteous anger. Regardless of whether or not her suffering resulted from her own choices or the choices of someone else, Bathsheba could choose how to respond.

After the loss of her son, Bathsheba could have disappeared into the harem of David's wives in shame, never to be heard from again. However, this is not what happened. It is very possible the pain and suffering David and Bathsheba experienced together created a bond between them that was different from the bond David had with his other wives. Pain and suffering hurt, but God will always find a way to reconstruct something good when deconstruction threatens to destroy.

Upon hearing of his son's death, David, who had been fasting and praying to God for a reprieve, responded by ending his fast, taking a bath, and worshipping God. David's growth after enduring his own pain and suffering is apparent in that he still chose to worship God even after God carried out the consequence of David's sin. It's not uncommon for people who have experienced God's discipline to turn away from Him in anger. In other words, if God isn't going to do what they want Him to do and, instead, disciplines them for living life their own way, they want nothing to do with Him. But that's just not how it works.

To draw on the parenting comparison again, when we discipline our children for a grave offense, they don't turn away from us in anger forever. They might for a little while, but usually they'll see that our discipline was intended for their own good. Hopefully, they never doubt our intense love, and it's even better when they someday realize we discipline them because we love them so much. David still petitioned God for a reprieve, but when God didn't relent, David could have chosen to turn away from Him in anger. Instead, David turned toward God because he understood God loved him and had chosen him—even if his prayers were not answered in the way he desired (2 Samuel 12:16).

Even better, when David's servants asked why he stopped fasting and mourning after the death of his son, he answered, "I will go to him, but he will not return to me" (2 Samuel 12:23). This belief that he would someday be reunited with his son gave David the stamina to get up off the ground, clean himself up, eat, and go to Bathsheba. Faith is what gets so many of us up off the ground and soldiering on— even when we live hour by hour and minute by minute. David was no different.

Then something really big happens. In 2 Samuel 12:24-25, we see that David goes to Bathsheba to comfort her. Here's what happens: "Then David comforted his wife Bathsheba, and he went to her and made love to her. She gave birth to a son, and they named him Solomon. The LORD loved him; and because the LORD loved him, he sent word through Nathan the prophet to name him Jedidiah."

There is so much more to this story, and I'm excited to tell you the rest, but we still have some other things to talk about before we get to that. God redeems David and comforts Bathsheba through the birth of a child who would become the great king Solomon. We all know you can never replace a child, and that's not what God was trying to do. Instead, by choosing Bathsheba to bear the next king, God told her she was seen. He removed her shame. He understood her pain and had a plan all along to redeem it. God revealed His own broken heart for what she had endured at the hand of someone else and brought beauty from ashes in a mighty way.

Through the birth of Solomon, God communicated to David that he had been forgiven. Atonement for his sin had been paid, and David could start anew. In the midst of persevering with faith through the death of his son, all along God had planned for Solomon to be born to David and Bathsheba. Beauty from ashes. Yes, I'll keep talking about that beauty from ashes because it's a promise we need to hear often when we're suffering.

David and Bathsheba both could have given their anger permission to turn them away from God. My, how history would be different if they had made that choice! Instead, they chose to seek God rather than run from Him. They did not allow their shame to overtake them and win. And if it seems like we're still talking a lot about shame, you're correct. Shame, anger, comparison, and fear are all so intertwined, it's nearly impossible to talk about one without the other.

Living anger-free is living drama-free.
Living drama-free is living peace-full.
Living peace-full is living free. Living free
is God's goal for each of us.

As with shame, when we feel anger rising up, it's helpful to trace it back to the root. What's causing me to react this way? What do I really fear? Is this shame disguised as anger? When we can answer these questions, then we are ready to take positive action in the care and handling of our anger—before it handles us.

When our anger handles us, we give it the upper hand; we allow it to control us rather than controlling it ourselves. It's true there are some things we cannot control. As the child of an alcoholic, one of my favorites is the Serenity Prayer, which says, "God, grant me the serenity to accept the things I cannot change, the courage to change the things I can, and the wisdom to know the difference." When faced with something we cannot control, we get to choose how we respond; and responding by handling our anger is not only what God desires for us but also what we really desire too. When push comes to shove, does anyone really want to be angry? There may be some for whom their anger is a part of how they want to portray themselves, but that's really just a façade of shame. Living anger-free is living drama-free. Living drama-free is living peace-full. Living peace-full is living free. Living free is God's goal for each of us. Sweet freedom, indeed.

However, not allowing ourselves to be handled by our anger is a lot easier said than done. How do we handle our anger before it handles us? To quote one of my favorite authors, Karen Ehman, we "pause before we pounce."[2] We sit down for a moment, take a deep breath, and pray. We seek compassion for the person causing our anger and try to see the situation from that person's perspective (except in the case of abuse). We run through the "Ten Test"—that is, will this matter in ten minutes? Ten days? Ten months? Ten years? We talk to someone, which brings our anger to the light. Here's the thing: if we can handle our anger before it handles us, we will stop it from turning into shame.

Whenever I feel my blood starting to boil, I think of the wisdom of James 1:19: "My dear brothers and sisters, take note of this: Everyone should be quick to listen, slow to speak and slow to become angry." Quick to listen. Slow to speak. Slow to become angry. This takes tremendous self-control, but we can do it, friend, because we can do hard things.

Take a look at that same verse in *The Message*: "Post this at all the intersections, dear friends: Lead with your ears, follow up with your tongue, and let anger straggle along in the rear. God's righteousness doesn't grow from human anger. So throw all spoiled virtue and cancerous evil in the garbage. In simple humility, let our gardener, God, landscape you with the Word, making a salvation-garden of your life."

Don't you just love the visual of our anger straggling along in the rear? Good riddance, cancerous evil. There's a not-so-new Master Gardener in town, and He's far more powerful than you.

Turning to God

Prayerfully read and meditate on the following Scriptures:

Psalm 37:8-9
Proverbs 15:1
Proverbs 29:22 (New Living Translation, if possible)
James 4:1-2

Questions for Reflection or Discussion

1. Reflect on righteous anger versus sin anger. What are the differences between the two? Why do you think God excuses righteous anger? How can righteous anger become sin anger? How does sin anger affect us long-term? Why do you think God was not angry with Bathsheba but instead focused on David?

2. Our words can either provoke anger or diffuse anger. Read Proverbs 15:1. Think of a situation in which you used harsh words instead of gentle answers. What was the outcome? If you had chosen to use gentle answers, do you think the situation would have been different? Why or why not?

3. James 4:1-2 suggests that fights and quarrels between people really stem from the selfish desires we all possess. Do you agree with James? Why or why not? How can our own selfishness lead us to sin anger?

4. According to Psalm 37:8-9, what leads to evil? What happens to those who are evil? What happens to those who hope in the Lord? What is one strategy you can use today if you find yourself becoming angry?

5. I like the New Living Translation's wording of Proverbs 29:22 because it's very clear what happens to those who struggle

with sin anger: "An angry person starts fights; a hot-tempered person commits all kinds of sin." Our anger often leads to sin, and sin leads to evil. Have you seen evidence of this in your own life? What was the result? How would the situation have been different if anger was diffused?

6. Prayer works. It's true that sometimes our prayers are not answered in the way our heart desires; however, we can still petition to the Lord and He will hear our prayers. David petitioned to the Lord by fasting and remaining faithful, yet his son still died. What did David do afterward? Why is this important? What was the first thing he chose to do right after attending to his physical needs of food and rest? Do you think this would be important to God? Why or why not?

7. How might this story end if Bathsheba chooses to remain angry? Would this be pleasing to God? Even though Bathsheba is without sin, she can choose how she will react. How would living with intense anger hinder her life? How would releasing it help?

6

Turning Away from Comparison

We won't be distracted by comparison if we're captivated with purpose.

—Bob Goff

ot too long ago I found myself in a situation where I felt trapped. Honestly, I didn't see a way out. If I made one choice, I would affect one group of people. If I made another, I would affect another group. Feeling deadlocked is not a good thing for a girl who loves to walk in freedom. Nothing makes me start to panic more than feeling suffocated, stuck, and smothered.

Chewing this over in my mind while shuttling my tweens and teens to yet another event, I looked up during a beautiful Midwest sunset to see geese flying in their typical V-formation. They were so beautiful and, yes, so free. Now here's where it gets hilarious, friend. I actually found myself envying these geese. I mean, really. I did. Then I began to think of all the people I knew who lived in freedom like this. But God chose that moment to tell me a not-always-so-evident truth. "How do you know they are free?" He nudged. And the truth is, I didn't. I had also made some pretty strong assumptions about people who seem so carefree but maybe really aren't. I hope they are, but it's possible my perception doesn't match reality. Oh, how that gets me in trouble. When we compare ourselves to others, we make a whole lot of assumptions that oftentimes are not anywhere close to the truth.

Perhaps you know something about comparing yourself to someone else too. It has been said that comparison is the thief of joy. Yet, as women, we give the thief access to our most precious possessions far too often. Comparison crept into the world when the serpent asked Eve, "Did God really say, 'You must not eat from any tree in the garden'?" (Genesis 3:1). The enemy placed doubt, and when we compare ourselves, we're doubting ourselves.

In 1954, psychologist Leon Festinger created a term for when we determine our self-worth based on how we compare to those around us: social comparison theory.[1] Interestingly, we don't tend to compare ourselves to others who are not in our area of work, interest, or talent. For example, as a writer, I sometimes struggle with comparing myself to other writers, but I never struggle with comparing myself to people who do crafts because Lord knows I am terrible at crafts. We are all given certain responsibilities, and these responsibilities can only be carried out by those chosen to do so. Galatians 6:4-5 says, "Each one should test their own actions. Then they can take pride in themselves alone, without comparing themselves to someone else, for each one should carry their own load." Everyone carries a different load. They're all heavy, but they're all also custom-made just for us.

The Message translation of Galatians 6:4-5 says it like this: "Make a careful exploration of who you are and the work you have been given, and then sink yourself into that. Don't be impressed with yourself. Don't compare yourself with others. Each of you must take responsibility for doing the creative best you can with your own life." If we unpack that one line at a time, Paul is telling us that we need to assess who we are and what God has called us to do. Once we've established that, we commit ourselves to this cause but without developing a big head. Don't look sideways at others and compare, but, instead, look up to God and do the best with what He has called you, and only you, to do.

When we are in the midst of our own pain and suffering, it's so easy to look at others who seem to have this life thing figured out and envy their wisdom. We wonder why we got such a raw deal while they get to coast. We lament and cry out for a fast-forward button that doesn't exist. We want to scream, "No fair!" even though we know quite well life was never promised to be fair. Life is promised to be eternal if we choose to follow Jesus, but it was never promised to be fair.

One of my favorite commercials features a client questioning a tattoo artist about his competency. The tattoo artist responds with, "Stay in your lane!" which always makes me giggle. But really, this essentially is what Paul is telling the Galatians. Cultivate the responsibilities God has entrusted to you and focus only on your specific load. Stay in your lane. Don't look sideways.

First Chronicles 3 lists David's descendents spanning over thirty generations. Within these Scriptures, all seven of David's wives are named in the order in which they became his wives: Ahinoam, Abigail, Maacha, Haggith, Abital, Eglah, and Bath-shua (Bathsheba). The Bible is again silent about how Bathsheba may have felt after losing her son and being David's last wife. However, since David did indeed have seven wives, I think it's safe to assume there was probably some comparing going on.

Let's just be real: I don't think any of us would disagree that comparison is something that plagues most women. I'm sure men sometimes struggle with comparison too, but I think the enemy often uses comparison among women because he understands the power of its destruction. When he questioned Eve in the garden, he was essentially encouraging Eve to compare herself with God. "Who has more power—you or God?" he implied. "Doesn't God want what's best for you? He must not if He won't allow you to eat this sweet and tasty fruit." See how this works? Lies, lies, lies. But they are so easy to believe if we aren't paying attention.

It's perfectly natural to compare ourselves to others when we're suffering, but it's also horribly unhealthy to give those comparisons any power. I don't think we can talk about comparison and not discuss Rachel and Leah, two feuding sisters featured in Genesis 29–35. Both women were suffering in their own way and yet were staunch rivals. Jacob fell in love with Rachel, his first cousin, when he met her at the well after traveling to find his uncle, Laban. Laban was Rachel's father, who welcomed Jacob to his home and gave him work. When he asked for Rachel's hand in marriage, Laban agreed. But then he pulled one over on Jacob and tricked him into marrying Leah, Rachel's less attractive older sister. Jacob was eventually allowed to marry Rachel, but that was only the beginning of an ongoing feud between the sisters—both married to the same man.

On the one hand, because God knew Leah was not loved by Jacob as much as Rachel, He blessed her with the ability to bear many children—specifically, many sons, which was considered very impressive back in those days. On the other hand, Rachel was barren, or so it seemed. While she eventually gave birth to two sons, she struggled with infertility for a long time. Rachel's infertility led to intense envy and bitterness toward Leah, while Leah envied Rachel because of her husband's preference for her. The two sisters go back and forth for several chapters in Genesis, and I confess I just want to yell, "Enough already!" to them both.

I wonder how history would have been different if Rachel and Leah just tried to make the best of a less-than-ideal situation. I wonder what would have happened if they'd chosen to love and support each other rather than tear each other down. And I wonder if they could have alleviated their anger, bitterness, and resentment by simply refusing to compare themselves to each other and, instead, valued each other's strengths. Rachel eventually gave birth to a son, Joseph, and another, Benjamin; however, she died while giving birth to Benjamin. If Rachel had not been so consumed by keeping up with Leah, would she have lived a longer life? We'll never know.

If we forget to stay in our lane, we'll eventually have a head-on collision.

Not surprising, comparison leads to shame (you know we couldn't get through the chapter without bringing up the s-word again, right?), and sometimes leads to anger and fear as well. But since we know that shame is the only emotion that can attach to other emotions, then it's no shock that comparison and shame are dear, dear friends. When we compare ourselves with someone else, we begin to berate ourselves for not being like the object of our comparison. When we berate ourselves, we feel less than, hidden, and unworthy. When we feel less than, hidden, and unworthy, yes, that's shame.

Comparison can lead to anger in that we might even develop a sense of entitlement because why should someone else have what we want? Aren't we entitled to have what they have? If we forget to stay in our lane, we'll eventually have a head-on collision. Of course, at the root of comparison, anger, and shame is fear. We'll talk more about that in the next chapter, but until then, understand that these three work in tandem to derail, deconstruct, and depress.

Speaking of depression, researchers have discovered a correlation between time spent on social media and depression.[2] The more time you spend scrolling through feeds, the higher your chances of grabbing a case of the blues. Not necessarily shocking, I know. But if you're like me, sometimes we need to state the obvious before we actually see it.

Now, I need to shoot straight and say I have a love-hate relationship with social media. I think it's a great tool for encouraging, supporting, and loving other people. How we choose to use this tool rests upon our shoulders. Like all tools, it can be used for good or it can be used for not-so-good. A hammer is a great tool for hammering nails but not so good for tightening screws. The same is true of social media.

It's also important to pay attention to how we are feeling as we scroll through our social media feeds. In a study conducted by the University of Michigan, it was discovered that the more time participants spent scrolling through Facebook, the higher their reports of general unhappiness.[3] The less time spent on Facebook, the happier and content most people felt. In fact, it's recently been discovered that social media is actually addictive. If we receive several likes and comments, we keep going back for more. If we aren't feeling validated in real life, then we may look to social media for validation. And this is a very slippery slope. When we base our identity and sense of self-worth on something that can so easily be taken away, we're setting ourselves up for eventual heartbreak.

Sometimes it's difficult to remember that when we make comparisons based on what we see on social media, we are stacking ourselves up against someone else's highlight reel. These highlight reels are the best parts of their lives, often made snazzier because they're on camera. Friends on social media usually just want to show you their pretty front porch. You won't see a lot of messy living rooms on Facebook or Instagram. So if we are standing in our messy living room while looking at someone else's pretty front porch, well then the comparison train leaves the station.

When we are in the midst of our own suffering, comparing ourselves to another's journey will make our pain sting even more.

Breaking free of the comparison trap requires some intentionality on our part. I used to allow other things to define who I am. My marriage. Wealth. Status. My relationships. All of these things can be taken away, like a house built on sand, ready to collapse at any moment.

Building our houses on solid rock, on the truth of who God says we are, begins to shut the comparison trap down. This doesn't mean we won't sometimes still struggle, because we're human. But when we forget, we can remind ourselves of who we are according to Jesus. We can read Scripture. Take a walk. Remind ourselves that we're standing in our messy living rooms looking at someone else's pretty front porch. We can take naps. We can call a friend. Or read a book. Go for a run. Whatever allows you to tend to your soul, do it when the comparison trap threatens to snap. If we want to make positive changes, it starts with first agreeing to be good to yourself. Self-grace is imperative and yet it's hard for some of us, isn't it? Healing through our pain and suffering is not an easy journey, and it requires our full effort and intentionality—an effort that is so worth it in the end.

Turning to God

Prayerfully read and meditate on the following Scriptures:

Psalm 139:13-14
John 21:19-23
Acts 17:26
1 Peter 1:2

Questions for Reflection or Discussion

1. One of my favorite stories of comparison in Scripture is the story of Peter asking about what John would do in John 21:19-23. Jesus lovingly reminds him that what he asks John to do doesn't really matter. Read through these verses again. Is there a phrase that resonates with you? How do you feel when you read this story? How does this relate to comparison?

2. Assess your own feelings while scrolling through your social media feeds. Do you feel encouraged, loved, and supported, or do you feel sad, anxious, and depressed? Do you need to change any of your social media habits and behaviors? What advice would you give someone who is new to using social media—or someone who struggles with comparison while using it?

3. Read Psalm 139:13-14. Who does this Scripture say created us? What does it say about His creation? Why did God choose to make us all different? How do those differences help the kingdom of God?

4. How do you think David's wives, including Bathsheba, might have compared themselves to one another? Why?

5. Acts 17:26 states that God chose when and where we would each be born and live. How does this relate to comparing

ourselves with others? Now read 1 Peter 1:2. What is our purpose? How can this look different for each of us?

6. As I dive deeper into the life of Bathsheba, I find myself wondering if she ever struggled with comparing her old life with her new one. If she did, what do you think some of her particular struggles might have been? (I'm assuming Bathsheba's new life is a lot more complicated than the simple life she once led as the only wife of Uriah.)

7. Have you ever grieved the loss of a previous life you once had before there was an unexpected turn? Why do you think it is important to grieve the loss of an old life? What action steps can be taken to accept the "new" life?

$$\sim 7 \sim$$

Turning Away from Fear

> You gain strength, courage, and confidence by every experience in which you really stop to look fear in the face. You are able to say to yourself "I lived through this horror. I can take the next thing that comes along."
> —Eleanor Roosevelt, *You Learn by Living*

When I'm writing a book, social media is a great way to gather insights from the community found on my Facebook author page. I ask readers' opinions on different topics ranging from the trivial to the intense, but none has stirred more responses than when I inquired about fear. I specifically asked readers to weigh in on fear in general—that is, how it has affected their lives and how they manage it or have worked through it. All I can say is, I was not quite prepared for the slew of responses those questions garnered.

If you've ever had an anxious thought, you've experienced fear. If worry is a stronghold for you, you've experienced fear. And if you can't stop thinking about what could possibly happen, you've experienced fear. My Aunt Nancy uses an acronym for fear I just love. "Fear is just Future Events Appearing Real, sis," she says. Isn't this the truth? So much of our fear is based on events that may or may not ever happen.

Fear steals reason, logic, and truth from even the most level-headed person.

My husband and I recently experienced a difficult valley in our marriage. Tough moments and hard conversations were pretty much the daily norm, and the emotional intensity of this wore both of us down to the point of exhaustion. There were so many days I wanted to just walk out the front door and never look back. Have you ever felt that way? I actually found myself wondering what would happen if I got in my car and just kept driving.

The thing about fear is that our first response is to run. No, actually, sprint. We are creatures of comfort, and there's nothing comfortable about fear. Once it starts to creep in, the fight-or-flight response takes over and we say things we shouldn't, do things we shouldn't, and believe lies we shouldn't. We may even know better, but then fear steals reason, logic, and truth from even the most level-headed person. Fear cannot, and should not, ever be trusted.

In fact, if we trace every negative emotion we feel to the root, chances are very likely we'll end at the doorstep of fear. For example, I recently experienced anxiety about the confidence of one of my children. For two days, I wondered what I could do to build him up. I worried about what I had done to make him this way. I lost sleep and snapped at the people I love the most. After two days of this crippling anxiety, I was struck with a moment of clarity.

I was worried about my son's lack of self-confidence. This worry was really just a mask for the fear I felt about how this would affect his entire life. I went from zero to sixty in thirty seconds and before I knew it, I'd created a fear-based photo of my adult son, unable to function in society. Did I mention he is currently twelve years old? First of all, this is not an accurate snapshot because my son was just having a moment of low self-esteem. Everyone has them, and it certainly doesn't mean we're doomed for life. But when it comes to your children, well, logic isn't always one of the ingredients. Yet when I recognized what was going on and decided to no longer give the enemy the upper hand on my thoughts, I was able to see the lack of logic and truth behind this anxiety.

One question I like to ask my readers when I'm researching is: "What comment, on this topic, would make you want to throw this book across the room?" I feel pretty strongly about being real and not delivering trite, Christian answers all wrapped up with a pretty bow. Sometimes life is just hard because this isn't our eternal home. Our citizenship is in heaven (Philippians 3:20). We're visitors. Visitors don't always have the security and comfort of home. Remember when we talked about John 16:33 in chapter one? In this world we will have trouble, but thankfully, that's not the end. Jesus has overcome the world. He has the last word, and He wins.

One reader responded to the book-throwing question by saying, "Don't tell me to just stop feeling fear. I know I shouldn't feel fear, but I still do. Recognize that I feel it, and tell me how to work through it. Don't tell me it's a lack of faith. I've already dealt with the shame of that. That makes my fear worse. Just tell me that I'm not alone and that I can overcome this."

Oh, girl. You are absolutely not alone. And there's no doubt in my mind that you can overcome this. I'm not sure fear will ever completely go away until we are fully sanctified, but I know there are ways to manage our anxieties and fears because, again, we are more than conquerors. We can conquer this fear, just as Bathsheba conquered hers.

Now this is where it gets really good, friends. This is the part I've been most excited to share with you because it reveals so much of Bathsheba's healing and progress. But before we get there, let's go over what happened prior to her display of courage. Amnon and Absalom,

David's two oldest sons, died before King David did, thus leaving Adonijah as the next chronological heir to the throne. As David lay on his deathbed, Adonijah acquired chariots and a rather large entourage in preparation for the celebration in which he would declare himself king. This assumption could seem rather innocent given the fact that he was indeed the oldest living son, but suspiciously, he didn't invite his brother Solomon or any of Solomon's supporters. I smell a rat.

Adonijah's omission confirms the fact that he did indeed know he was usurping the throne from Solomon. Although it is not specifically mentioned in Scripture, at some point David made an oath to Bathsheba that he would declare Solomon as his heir, and Nathan was also aware of this agreement (1 Kings 1:13). However, when Adonijah began planning his pomp and circumstance, David remained silent, thus possibly causing his eldest living son to believe he had his father's approval.

We don't know if David remained silent because of his mental state or just sheer exhaustion because, let's face it, the man had seen some drama in his life and it's possible he was simply over it all. Enter Nathan, the same prophet who spoke to David after he first slept with Bathsheba and then had her husband killed. If you remember, Nathan cleverly used a parable to reveal David's sin. God wasn't very happy with David, and the fact that Nathan had the courage to speak boldly of this to the king led David to have great respect for Nathan. King David obeyed whatever Nathan said, probably out of fear of what would result if he didn't. He understood Nathan to be a messenger from God who was not to be doubted or disrespected. Personally, Nathan is one of my favorites in the Bible. Don't you just love how he's so committed to truth and doing the right thing?

Nathan understood what was at stake for both Bathsheba and Solomon if Adonijah did indeed become king. Since they were not invited to Adonijah's self-declaration-to-the-throne ceremony, it was pretty obvious Adonijah knew Solomon had been promised to succeed David. Clearly, Adonijah was just trying to pull a fast one over on everyone before David passed away. He would have succeeded if it weren't for that pesky Nathan filling Bathsheba in on his sneaky plan.

Another reason to love Nathan is his integrity and motivation to protect both Bathsheba and Solomon. Nathan understood that if Adonijah were to become king, he would have Bathsheba and Solomon killed—and very likely anyone who supported them. This would conveniently remove any threat to the throne, and, just like that, Adonijah would reign. But what happens next is where we can stand in awe of Bathsheba's strength, courage, and growth.

In 1 Kings 1:12-14, Nathan advises Bathsheba to talk to David. After telling her about Adonijah, he says,

> Now then, let me advise you how you can save your own life and the life of your son Solomon. Go in to King David and say to him, "My lord the king, did you not swear to me your servant: 'Surely Solomon your son shall be king after me, and he will sit on my throne'? Why then has Adonijah become king?" While you are still there talking to the king, I will come in and add my word to what you have said.

This is big, friend, because back then it was considered risky to approach a king on his deathbed—even if you were his wife. I'm thinking Bathsheba might have been feeling some fear. And don't you just love how Nathan told her he would back her up? I'm sure that helped alleviate some of her fear, just like it does for us when we know someone has our back. Yet I'm pretty certain she felt a little apprehensive before approaching King David, husband or not.

When we are faced with something that scares the pants off of us, one of the best things we can do for ourselves is to pause for a moment and reflect on our fear. Recognize what is at the root of what we're feeling, decide how to proceed, and do so carefully. Fear can bring out behaviors in us that aren't always consistent with who we are. In fact, most of my less-than-shining moments occurred because I was feeling fearful of something. However, Bathsheba understood what she was facing, and while she might have been terrified, she proceeded with wisdom and courage.

So Bathsheba went to see the aged king in his room, where Abishag the Shunammite was attending him. Bathsheba bowed down, prostrating herself before the king (1 Kings 1:15-16).

While Bathsheba had a more casual relationship with David than most of his closest followers, she still chose to pause and reflect on how to best proceed. By doing so, Bathsheba realized that the most effective way to communicate with David was to show extreme respect and approach him as a servant does her master. What if she had chosen to barge into David's chambers and demand he see things her way? I know from experience that when we handle delicate situations like this, the end result isn't usually what we want. It's possible Bathsheba's self-control could have changed the course of history.

When King David saw Bathsheba prostrate on the ground before him, he asked why she was there. She answered,

> My lord, you yourself swore to me your servant by
> the LORD your God: "Solomon your son shall be king
> after me, and he will sit on my throne." But now
> Adonijah has become king, and you, my lord the
> king, do not know about it. He has sacrificed great
> numbers of cattle, fattened calves, and sheep, and
> has invited all the king's sons, Abiathar the priest
> and Joab the commander of the army, but he has
> not invited Solomon your servant. My lord the king,

> the eyes of all Israel are on you, to learn from you
> who will sit on the throne of my lord the king after
> him. Otherwise, as soon as my lord the king is laid
> to rest with his ancestors, I and my son Solomon will
> be treated as criminals. (1 Kings 1:17-21)

Bathsheba didn't only reflect on how to best approach David. She also reflected on how to best communicate with David. In verse 20, Bathsheba informs David that all of Israel is watching him in anticipation of who he will crown as his heir. Remember when David tried to cover up his sin after impregnating Bathsheba? He did so because of shame, yes. But surely he also did so because he was concerned about his image, and Bathsheba must have understood this. It seems she used this knowledge to seek his attention and remind him that all of Israel was watching and expected him to do the right thing. Well played, Bathsheba.

Soon after Bathsheba spoke with David, Nathan arrived and confirmed her story. Like Bathsheba, Nathan obviously reflected on how to best communicate with David because in verse 27, he asks, "Is this something my lord the king has done without letting his servants know who should sit on the throne of my lord the king after him?"

When we diffuse fear, we infuse hope.

Nathan did not accuse, placing David on the defensive. He simply asked if it was, perhaps, an oversight that David's most trusted advisors were not aware of this change in plans.

Next, David asks for Bathsheba to join them and says, "As surely as the LORD lives, who has delivered me out of every trouble, I will surely carry out this very day what I swore to you by the LORD, the God of Israel: Solomon your son shall be king after me, and he will sit on my throne in my place" (vv. 29-30).

A delicate situation, diffused by pausing in the face of fear and trusting God to handle the details. Hard to do? Absolutely. Impossible? Clearly not. When we diffuse fear, we infuse hope. When we refuse to fall for the enemy's schemes, we transfer our fear from ourselves to him. The enemy trembles when faced with the power of God and hates when we don't choose to be scared anymore.

Furthermore, Bathsheba's willingness to approach David exemplifies her own personal growth. She contemplated how to best speak to her husband, which exhibits wisdom. She summoned the courage to say it all. And wisdom plus courage equals loyalty to her son, who was the rightful heir. Without Bathsheba's courage to speak up, Adonijah would have become king, and very likely, Solomon and Bathsheba would have been killed. The first temple in Jerusalem would not have been built by Solomon. The Book of Proverbs would be vastly different—if it would even exist at all. And no Song of Songs. While all scripture comes from God (2 Timothy 3:16), Solomon was a very important vessel God used greatly. His death at a young age would have had a vast effect on the lineage of Jesus (Matthew 1:1-17).

Ever since I was a young girl, one of my favorite Christmas specials was *A Charlie Brown Christmas*. First of all, I don't care how many new digital advancements we've all seen since this program's debut more than fifty years ago, it's still a hard one to beat. Who doesn't love the Peanuts gang? And who doesn't love that sweet Linus who always carries around his security blanket? A few years ago it was brought to my attention that there is only one time in all of the Peanuts' episodes when Linus actually drops his security blanket. This moment had to be big because that security blanket was everything to Linus. But in the famous scene in which he is sharing the verses of Luke detailing the birth of Jesus, Linus drops his blanket when he recites "Fear not."[1] Linus no longer needs the false security found in anything other than Jesus. Jesus chases out fear. Fear not.

One of my friends and I were talking about how fear kept her in an unhealthy relationship for a long time. "I didn't have a relationship with Jesus, so I believed the fear," she said. This stopped me dead in my tracks because this was my experience as well, but I had never given it much thought. However, as I started to think more about this, I was reminded of 1 John 4:16, which simply states, "God is love." Verse 18 then states, "There is no fear in love. But perfect love drives out fear." Perfect love is God, friend. And that perfect love literally drives out fear. It is through our relationship with Jesus in which we stop believing the lies that produce fear.

Fear never, ever comes from God and always comes from the enemy. How do we know? Second Timothy 1:7 says so: "For God gave us a spirit not of fear but of power and love and self-control" (ESV). God doesn't dole out stuff that will clip our wings. He gives us gifts that will allow us to reach the full potential He so desires for us. He gives us power through the Holy Spirit. He gives us love, which is Himself. And He gives us enough strength to control ourselves.

I'm so thankful Bathsheba didn't cower to her fear. Solomon eventually became a very wise, respected king who wrote most of the Book of Proverbs. In fact, King Lemuel was believed to have actually been King Solomon under a different name and the author of Proverbs 31. This chapter is best known as the "perfect woman's" chapter because in it, the king shares wisdom from his mother. His mother, of course, was Bathsheba. A woman who overcame her shame, fought against fear, and embraced courage—a bold move that changed the course of history.

Turning to God

Prayerfully read and meditate on the following Scriptures:

Psalm 23:4
Psalm 46:1
John 14:27

Questions for Reflection or Discussion

1. Take a moment to assess your own anxieties and concerns. Trace each negative emotion to the root. Do you find fear? How can you remove this fear? What will you have to do? How does Psalm 46:1 offer you encouragement?

2. Read John 14:27. What does Jesus leave with us? How is the peace of Jesus different from the peace the world offers? What else does Jesus tell us not to do?

3. Why do you think it takes courage to remove fear from our lives?

4. Psalm 23:4 says, "Even though I walk through the darkest valley, I will fear no evil, for you are with me; your rod and your staff, they comfort me." The shadow of death can be any period of suffering we endure. Why do you think it is so difficult to trust God when we are in the shadow of death? What does God promise us in this verse? You might even want to write this down so you can remember it—it's that good.

5. Nathan instructed Bathsheba on how to best approach David. How do you think this influenced David? How would it have been different if she had charged into his bedroom and demanded he make a profession that Solomon was to be the king? Reread 1 Kings 1:17-21. Now, read Proverbs 15:1-2. How does Bathsheba's approach correspond to the wisdom

found in these Proverbs verses? How can we apply this to our own lives?

6. Wisdom + Courage = Loyalty. Reflect on this for a moment. Bathsheba's wisdom of how to approach David, combined with her courage to do so at all, exhibited her loyalty to her son and her commitment to positive change. How is wisdom and courage the best way to achieve positive change?

7. Fear never comes from God. Since he gives us a spirit of power, love, and self-control (2 Timothy 1:7 ESV), we can conclude that *courage* comes from God. Why do you think God placed this sense of justice so heavily on Bathsheba's heart? Why was it important for her to obey?

Part 2

Moving Forward

❦ 8 ❦

Permission to Grieve

No one ever told me that grief felt so like fear.
—C. S. Lewis, *A Grief Observed*

I think most parents would agree that losing a child, even an adult child, is our worst nightmare. It defies natural order and just plain shouldn't happen. Yet we all know that just because something shouldn't happen doesn't mean it won't. One of my dearest friends, Karri, lost her six-year-old daughter, Caroline, to cancer twelve years ago. Karri spent two years with Caroline in a hospital two states away that specialized in her specific cancer. After Caroline passed, my sweet friend felt empty and disoriented. For two years she had lived away from the rest of her family, fought for her daughter, and remained hopeful that Caroline would beat this aggressive cancer.

While I agree with C. S. Lewis that grief feels so much like fear, it isn't. Grief is what's left after you put your heart out there and love something so fiercely you don't care if it's taken away, because it's worth the fight. It takes courage to do that. However, when it's over, the heaviness that sits upon your shoulders feels like the burden of fear, but it's actually love. You see, while fear is something that erases and takes away, grief is something that adds to our story and makes us who we are. It makes us real, just like the velveteen rabbit.

My children are intense animal lovers, and one day my son mentioned how much he loved elephants. I have always been fascinated with elephants as well. So we began researching facts, and I stumbled upon something beautiful. When a female elephant loses a calf, the other elephants in the herd come alongside her and encircle the body of her baby. This display of support for the mother has been known to last more than twelve hours. During these twelve hours, other elephants gently stroke the mother, offering the comfort of their presence. Life stands still. The most important thing during this time is to comfort, console, and care for the grieving mother.

A few years ago when a calf died on a coffee farm in west India, a grieving herd had to be dispersed after twelve hours by park rangers. One ranger reported he could hear the herd trumpeting for miles and hours following. Specialists have also stated that mother elephants often grieve the hardest. They've been known to spend days with the body of their deceased calf, and it's not uncommon for mothers to attempt to carry the body with them when they must leave. Andrea Crosta, Director of the Elephant Action League, said, "Elephants press together and console each other, grieving for the loss. You can see the suffering on their face and in their posture. They will watch over their relative for days and make mournful-sounding noises, sometimes defending the body against predators."[1]

I think maybe elephants understand something we don't. When someone is grieving, it's natural to want to say or do something to make the pain just go away. While this arises from a position of compassion, sometimes our compassion does the opposite of what we had hoped. Oftentimes in our attempt to alleviate and help the hurting move past their grief, we say and do things that hurt them even more. As a species always striving for comfort, we are uncomfortable with allowing someone to simply sit in their grief. We say things like, "This was all just part of God's plan," or "Everything happens for a reason," or "Now he/

she is an angel looking over you." And we mean well, really. However, statements like this often minimize grief. Usually, the one grieving doesn't want to hear about God's plan, why their loss happened, or that their loved one has joined the heavenly angels. The grieving just want permission to grieve. There may come a time when those statements will encourage rather than discourage, but grief cannot be rushed.

Grief is a fickle emotion, making you feel fine one moment and not-so-fine the next. It can be conjured out of nowhere by a song or a scent or a conversation. Grief doesn't really ever go away; we just learn to manage it. Karri once told me of a well-meaning person who asked when she thought she would be "over" Caroline's death. "Never," she answered matter-of-factly. "I'll never be over her death. I'll just learn to manage my grief and adjust to the new normal. We don't have a choice."

Once at a party another person critically told Karri she was "just so different" since Caroline's passing. "I am different," she responded. "I'll never be the same." Of course she won't be the same. A huge part of her is missing, but, fortunately, this doesn't mean she has to live the rest of her life in sorrow. Eventually, we learn to manage our grief, fully live again, and even experience joy. A piece of our heart will be different, but usually it's the part that allows us to love others even more fiercely and unselfishly. Grief separates our lives into a before and after, a then and now. The after or now is almost always a more compassionate and deeper version of who we were before or then.

We don't know the full extent of Bathsheba's grief, but we do know that mothers are hardwired to care for their young and, therefore, grieve for their young. I think we can assume that Bathsheba, like an elephant mother, grieved deeply for the loss of her young son. Compounded by the fact that this consequence wasn't because of her own choices, I'm sure her grief also included anger and, at times, even fear.

We see evidence of David's grief in 2 Samuel 12:16-17: "David pleaded with God for the child. He fasted and spent the nights lying in sackcloth on the ground. The elders of his household stood beside him to get him up from the ground, but he refused, and he would not eat any food with them."

But when David received word that his son had died, he tended to himself and, as we are told in verse 24, went to comfort Bathsheba. Even though we don't need to be told that a mother would grieve for her child, this verse proves she did.

It's also important to note that grief is not only reserved for those who have lost loved ones to physical death. Sometimes losing loved ones comes in the form of divorce. Or a broken, irreparable friendship. Or severed ties with a child or parent. In the end, grief is about losing a piece of our hearts, and any kind of loss can lead to grief.

Recently I experienced a deep betrayal. This was a shock as I thought this person was a reliable and close friend for life. I'm always surprised by the people who turn out to be friends for a season instead of friends for life, but this one left me particularly wounded and sad. I just didn't see it coming, and I grieved. I grieved the lost friendship I thought we had, I grieved not being heard, and I grieved the fact that I was not important enough to this person to even warrant a discussion. Yet it was through this grief that I learned to be more careful with my heart in the face of friendship. Likewise, when I divorced my first husband almost twenty years ago, I grieved the death of our marriage. I grieved for the life we had planned. I grieved for the children I once imagined we would have. I grieved for a family I had envisioned for years that would never come to be.

Death wasn't in God's original plan when He created Adam and Eve. The wages of sin is death (Romans 6:23); and when Adam and Eve sinned in the garden, death entered the world. Sin is from the enemy and, therefore, so is death. The enemy would love nothing more than to see us be overcome with grief, leading to bitterness, anger, and resentment.

But God's ultimate goal for us is to draw closer and closer to Him. He wants us to love Him with a reckless love, trust Him with an illogical trust, and commit ourselves to Him with unwavering commitment— no matter what. It's in these periods of pain and suffering in which love, trust, and commitment to and for God builds. We become a bearer of His light, a vessel of His grace, and proof of His mercy. Yet I also know how unattainable this can seem when we are in the midst of intense grief. It can feel insurmountable, a mountain to traverse with a seventy-five-pound backpack strapped to our shoulders. But where there is despair, there is also hope.

When the unwelcome guest of grief knocks on our door, the best choice we can make is to invite him in. No, we won't want to do so. He's not a fun guest. He's messy, has inconvenient timing, and often overstays his welcome. However, forcing ourselves to feel the grief and not rush through it will lead to healing and hope that we often can't reach if we don't sit in it for a while. During these times we must be diligent with our own self-care by prioritizing rest, good nutrition, and a refusal to self-medicate. At times, it involves severing unhealthy relationships, which can add to our grief in the short-term but lead to a more complete healing in the long-term. Lastly, while it may feel like it takes too much energy to be with people, it's also important not to isolate ourselves while we are deep in grief. Laughter offers hope and eventually joy. Weeping may come for a night, "but a shout of joy comes in the morning" (Psalm 30:5 AMP).

Karri lost Caroline twelve years ago. Recently I asked her what grief felt like now, and she wrote this for me:

> Grief is like a rock. In the beginning it's a boulder, crushing and impossible to pick up. Once you realize it is yours to carry, you work on ways to deal with it. Time erodes this rock as you find people who help and learn to avoid

those that make it heavier. Some days it feels like a pebble in my pocket; other days it's huge and heavy.

I often compare grief to the African men and women who carry water jugs on their heads. With time and practice, we learn to carry it. There are always "tripping hazards" that catch me off guard. Smells, memories, and stress can send grief crushing down on me. I am much better now at accepting it. In the beginning, I flat-out refused to carry my grief. Once I accepted that, like it not, grief was here to stay, I learned how to cope with it. Now I put on my big-girl panties every day and hoist that water jug on top of my head. It is invisible to most, but it's always there and impacts every step I take.

Many of my friends have been unable to move through their grief because they don't have peace and hope. I thank God every night that He gave me these gifts and continues to bless me. I would sign up to do it all over again—every last second. Grief is the price of love, so I'll continue to adjust my stride as time passes and carry the load. It is bittersweet to see the kids that are Caroline's age. I so wonder where she would have fit in and what she would be doing. I miss her with every ounce of me.

I'm certain the same peace and hope God gave to Karri, He gave to Bathsheba. Like Karri, Bathsheba suffered great loss. I'm not sure there is a more painful loss to a mother's heart than the loss of a child. I know the pain felt unsurmountable at times. I know there are days when just getting out of bed is a feat. And I know there are moments when we celebrate making it through another hour, let alone a day. During these seasons of extreme grief, we can rest in the truth of Isaiah 54:10: " 'Though the mountains be shaken and the hills be removed, yet my unfailing love for you will not be shaken, nor my covenant of peace be removed,' says the LORD, who has compassion on you."

The strength to carry the weight of grief can only come from a compassionate God who offers His intense love, hope, and peace to carry us through.

Turning to God

Prayerfully read and meditate on the following Scriptures:

Psalm 18:30-33
Ecclesiastes 3:1-8
Romans 3:23
Revelation 21:4

Questions for Reflection or Discussion

1. How do you think fear and grief are similar? How are they different? Do you think Bathsheba experienced fear? Why or why not? How did she experience grief?

2. Read Revelation 21:4. How can this verse comfort those who are grieving? How could it possibly discourage them? Is it ever appropriate to share a verse like this with someone who is grieving? And if so, when?

3. Ecclesiastes 3:1-8 is one of my favorite scriptures. These verses offer such reassurance that our suffering will not last forever. Which one of the "times" listed most resonates with you right now? Why?

4. Besides the death of her husband Uriah, what else might Bathsheba have been grieving?

5. What are some compassionate things we can say to people who are grieving? What are hurtful things that might be said that could minimize their grief?

6. Read Psalm 18:30-33. What does God do for those who seek Him? According to these verses, what else does He provide?

7. I mentioned I had recently experienced a betrayal. How was Bathsheba betrayed? How do you think she will be offered hope? If you have experienced betrayal, how did this affect your heart? Read Romans 3:23. How does this apply to betrayal?

❧ 9 ❧

The Mind-Body Connection: Taking Care of You

Almost everything will work again if you unplug it for a few minutes—including you.
>   —Anne Lamott, "12 Truths I Learned
>   from Life and Writing"

*I*t's a fair assumption to say that if you're reading this book, you are a woman. And if you're a woman, then you probably know a thing or two about managing 752 things that must be done in five days. And if you know a thing or two about this, then it's also a fair assumption to say you are probably often tired, overwhelmed, and just plain empty. Can I get an amen? I feel you, sister.

Allow me to be candid and let you in on a little secret about myself: I can sometimes be a martyr. In other words, I put on my righteous hat and serve my family before myself but often to the point where I'm serving out of duty rather than desire. When this happens, I can become resentful and lament about how I'm the only one who does anything. And then before you know it, I convince myself I should win a medal for all the things I do for my family and, sometimes, other people. Good grief. Just typing this makes me cringe.

Two years ago my darling husband, the man who God chose to help sanctify me on this side of heaven, pointed this out. I hate being called out on my stuff, don't you? Because the thing is, when we are confronted about a behavior that is less than desirable, then we have to actually do something about it. At first I scoffed and became a martyr about my perceived lack of being a martyr. I think it's called denial. But in those small, still moments when I forced myself to get real, I realized it was true. I do become a martyr when I am overwhelmed and tired. And I get overwhelmed and tired *when I haven't prioritized taking care of myself.*

When my children were young, I didn't develop great self-care habits. As I'm typing this today, I'm staying at a quaint bed-and-breakfast type of Christian retreat center for four days. One of the other guests is a young mom with three children under the age of four. That was me. Except a big difference between this wise young mother and myself is that she prioritizes self-care. Doing so actually allows her to be the woman God called her to be—not out of duty but out of desire. Over breakfast this morning she shared with me her experience with post-partum depression and how this allowed her to finally understand how important self-care really is. I wish I had understood this better when I was her age.

When I start slipping into Natalie the Martyr, I know I need to refuel. I'm usually in need of a good nap or some time with my book in front of the fire. Yet it's often the first thing I'll push aside if there is too much going on—because who has time for that? Turns out, if we don't make time, the price will be a grouchy, snappy woman who makes her family feel badly for having basic needs. That's not the woman I want to be, and I know you don't want to be that woman either.

The Bible doesn't say much about how Bathsheba became so courageous and confident, but she obviously did some growing and healing in the years prior to her confrontation with David about

Solomon, and I am sure self-care played a role somewhere along the way. As I mentioned in chapter seven, Bathsheba emerges as a woman who is wise, courageous, and loyal. She didn't get that way by doing nothing. There had to have been a deepening of her faith through the trusting of God during the years following the birth of Solomon until the moments before David's death.

While technically this book is focused on Bathsheba, we can't discuss her without also discussing David. I particularly love how we are able to read about the events of his life in 1 and 2 Samuel and 1 Kings and read his responses to these events in the psalms he wrote at the same time. Psalm 32; 51; 86; and 122 were all written following David's affair with Bathsheba, the murder of her husband, his confrontation by Nathan, and his confession before God. Known as the "penetential psalms," these psalms, in which the author identifies his own sin and repents for his behavior, exhibit an understanding that his actions have led to the less-than-favorable situation he is facing. Penetential psalms usually include a cry for help, an update on the current undesirable consequence, and an appeal. They are humble in nature, which is critical if we seek God's forgiveness.[1]

When we are caring for ourselves, it's not just our physical needs we need to prioritize but our mental and spiritual needs as well. I firmly believe that when things aren't right in our relationship with God, things won't be right in our relationships with others. This is where self-care comes in. Sometimes, you might first need a nap to see that your relationship with God needs repair. But then you won't get very far down the self-care chain without tending to your relationship with the One who loves you more than any other.

Psalm 51 was written by David after Nathan confronted his sin. After David confesses to God, he then petitions for what he feels he needs to start anew. Verses 10 to 12 are of particular importance because it's what we need in order to get right with God again. We could probably take a cue from him too. Let's look at Psalm 51:10-12 together.

"Create in me a pure heart, O God, and renew a steadfast spirit within me" (Psalm 51:10). When we have been deceived by sin, there will always be distance in our relationship with God because sin separates us from Him. That was the plan. David is asking for a clean heart, as God promised He would do for his people in Jeremiah 24:7 and Ezekial 11:20. This clean heart would encourage His people to turn back to Him in obedience. This new heart will lead to a new spirit.

I also have to wonder—did Bathsheba pray this same prayer? Maybe not with the exact same words, but did she ask God to give her a new heart and spirit to accept her situation and new life? I think the answer is likely yes as I believe we see evidence of a new heart and a new spirit when Bathsheba confronts David in 1 Kings 1:17-21.

"Do not cast me from your presence or take your Holy Spirit from me" (Psalm 51:11). If we confess our sins to God with a humble heart, there is nothing we can do that would remove the Holy Spirit from us. Absolutely nothing. Ever. However, remember that David wrote these verses before Jesus lived, died, rose again, and sent the Holy Spirit to dwell within every believer. David became king after Saul, and because Saul turned away from God, God removed His spirit (1 Samuel 16:14). This may sound harsh, but Saul never confessed or humbled himself before God, which was the key difference between Saul and David. A humble spirit leads to forgiveness, grace, and mercy. And nothing can separate followers of Christ from God.

"Restore to me the joy of your salvation and grant me a willing spirit, to sustain me" (Psalm 51:12). Pure and true joy is found in our salvation because it's a mercy we don't deserve, purchased at a high price. A willing spirit is a humble spirit—a humility that will sustain us because God will never deny His grace from a humble follower.

Spending time in prayer is the best way to keep our relationship with God on track because prayer is simply having a conversation with Him. We can't build a relationship with someone we don't speak with regularly, and God is no different. He wants to hear our prayers. He wants to connect with us. He wants us to find rest in Him. He wants to know what's breaking our hearts—even though He already knows. God wants us to tell Him about why our hearts are broken.

This reminds me of when Jesus healed Bartimaeus in Mark 10:46-52. Bartimaeus was a blind man sitting on the side of the road when Jesus and His entourage passed by. "Jesus, son of David, have mercy on me!" he called to Jesus. When Jesus called him over, He didn't immediately heal Bartimaeus from his blindness, because He didn't assume this was what was ailing him. Instead, Jesus wanted to hear from Bartimaeus. In verse 51, Jesus simply asked, "What do you want me to do for you?"

God wants to hear what we want Him to do for us—what our needs are. He already knows, but He wants connection with us. It's true that what we want and what He wants may not be the same, but His way is better—even when we can't see it at first. One of my friends has a great expression that illustrates this perfectly. "I always pray for hamburger and God gives me steak," she says. Isn't that the truth? I have certainly feasted on steak when I was expecting hamburger too. Yet I also have to admit that at times, I've received mush, or nothing at all, instead of hamburger. God knows *what* is best for us and *when* it's best for us. Sometimes, the nothing we receive is because He wants us to focus on our relationship with Him and trust Him to eventually deliver that hamburger or steak. It's less about the tangible gift, or what we *get* out of our relationship with Him, and more about the actual relationship that matters most. A real, authentic relationship with God is better than the fanciest cuts of meat any day.

The restoration of our relationship with God is an important first step to our own self-care. Once our relationship has been restored, the next step is to pray for God to reveal what else we need for our soul. For some, it may be rest. For others, it might be time with friends. Maybe it's both. However, one of my friends firmly believes in scheduling time for herself each week. She may not even have specific plans, but she puts it in her calendar each week as her "weekly treat." She tells me, "Sometimes, my treat will be to go get a pedicure. Other times, I call a friend for a lunch date. Or sometimes I go for a walk somewhere scenic by myself and listen to good music. I always see things more clearly, feel things more accurately, and just feel more restored after my 'weekly treat.' And if I didn't put it on my calendar, I don't think I would do it."

Curious, I tried it out, and let me tell you, she's right! When I prioritized my own self-care by putting it in my calendar and protecting that precious time, I actually did it. Taking care of ourselves doesn't have to cost a penny. Some days I simply sit on my couch with a cup of tea and read a good book. It matters less about how you care for yourself and more that you just do it.

While self-care is important always, it's critically important when we are experiencing intense pain and suffering. Chronic fatigue is common among those who are grieving because the extreme amount of energy it takes to simply function in the world when our hearts are broken. But it's not only self-care we need to prioritize when we are hurting.

It's also important to have grace with yourself. Treat yourself with kindness. Sometimes I offer way more grace to other people than I am willing to extend to myself. I'm not sure why, because I am human and have human needs just like anyone else, but extending self-grace can sometimes be difficult. I'm guessing you might understand this as well because it's not an uncommon challenge among women.

We aren't sure how Bathsheba took care of herself while she was grieving the loss of her son, but I believe that at some point she must have discovered her own self-worth. Bathsheba was the wife of a respected king; therefore, we can assume she lived a very privileged life compared to most women. She lived in a beautiful palace, she likely had servants at her beck and call, and she didn't want for anything. Yet, wealth and power do not always equal peace. As was the case with David, powerful, wealthy people fall just as easily as those who are not. Temptation and sin do not discriminate; however, everyone needs to prioritize self-care because while it's trite, it's true: you aren't as effective as you could be if you don't take care of yourself.

Understanding our self-worth is at the root of self-care because when we recognize we are a person of value who must be cared for and loved, we are more likely to do it. And in case you didn't know, you are so valuable to God that He was willing to give the life of His only Son so He could be reunited with you again. I'd say you're worth it, sister.

Turning to God

Prayerfully read and meditate on the following Scriptures:

Psalm 51
Matthew 11:26-30 (*The Message*, if possible)
1 Corinthians 3:16

Questions for Reflection or Discussion

1. Is self-care difficult for you? Why or why not? Read Matthew 11:26-30. How does your soul respond to these verses?
2. Why is it important for our relationship with God to be tended before we take care of ourselves in other ways? How does a strained relationship with God affect other parts of our lives?
3. What is something you can do for yourself this week? Schedule it. Right now.
4. Read 1 Corinthians 3:16. According to this verse, why would self-care be important?
5. Read all of Psalm 51. What do you notice about David's posture before the Lord? Why is this important?
6. Since we don't really know what Bathsheba specifically did to take care of herself, let's just take a guess. What do you think she did for self-care? What spiritual practice did she add? Is prayer self-care? Why or why not?
7. What challenges do you think Bathsheba faced as the wife of the king? How do you think this affected Bathsheba spiritually and emotionally?
8. In this chapter, I confess to sometimes behaving like a martyr. Do you think Bathsheba ever confessed any character flaws in her own self? Why does humility ultimately set us free? Why do you think God values humility so much?

10

As Far As It Depends on You

> It isn't enough to talk about peace. One must believe in it. And it isn't enough to believe in it. One must work at it.
>
> —Eleanor Roosevelt

I'm so sick of being the one everyone walks all over. I feel like it's always my job to smooth everything out, to make it all OK, and sometimes I'm just tired of it," my friend confided to me in a cozy coffee shop one winter afternoon. Yes, she may have a bit of the same martyr syndrome I struggle with as well. She probably needs a good nap. But it's a legitimate concern because I bet you've felt like this at least once in your life as well. In our world of immediate-access drama, sometimes I wonder if conflict is leaking into our daily lives. In fact, I know it is. The television shows we watch are often laden with it, particularly between women. Not to mention, the longer we live, the higher our chances are of having at least one difficult relationship under our belts.

Let's just be real: relationships with other people can be hard. God didn't create all of us to be exactly the same, and this is a very, very good thing. But, at the same time, He created each of us to be wonderfully unique—so unique, in fact, that no two of us are the same. Which sometimes makes for very interesting and different perspectives of the same scene.

I wonder if there were times when Bathsheba looked at the current state of her life and wondered how on earth she got there. Anyone else? Here she was, married to Uriah, a respected warrior in David's army. They were likely planning to have children, as most women did during this time period. I'm sure Bathsheba had already envisioned her life going in one direction, but it actually didn't go that direction at all. Bathsheba's life took an unexpected turn to a place she never saw coming.

I also wonder how Bathsheba assimilated into her new life. As I've mentioned, I think it's safe to assume that her life as the wife of King David was completely different from her old life with Uriah. For starters, she was one of seven wives. Can you even imagine? Personally, I think that sounds like a hornet's nest. Going from being the only wife of one man to one of seven of another must have been quite the adjustment. Second, I'm sure there were more servants and comforts of a wealthy lifestyle than in her previous life. While this may sound great, it's still takes some getting used to—and isn't always all it's cracked up to be. Last, it's possible that Bathsheba may have entered this harem of wives with the label of the one who lured David, the reason for David's biggest mistake and regret. You and I know that's not really the truth, but remember that God didn't change His recipe for people. She might have been portrayed as the adulteress on more than one occasion.

At some point, Bathsheba had to reconcile a sense of peace within her soul. No, her life post-Uriah was not her fault. No, she was more of a victim than a coconspirator in sin. And no, she couldn't change a thing about what happened, and she couldn't change a thing about her new life, either. I'm sure there was more than one occasion when she felt just a bit powerless. However, the Bathsheba we see in 1 Kings 1 is a different Bathsheba from the one we met in 2 Samuel 11. Something happened along the way. Bathsheba had to decide how she would react to her situation, and it looks as though she chose peace.

There is a common misconception in our culture regarding those who seek peace. Peacemakers are not doormats. They are not pushovers. They are not weak. Peacemakers do not set their own needs aside. They do not compromise their own beliefs, thoughts, and actions for the sake of peace. Romans 12:18 gives us a good directive when it comes to our relationships: "As far as it depends on you, live at peace with everyone." Isn't this great advice? Wouldn't this be wonderful if we all could just live in peace? Except, reality. The key words here? *As far as it depends on you.*

On the one hand, peacemakers pursue peace. Even when they don't want to. Even when it's hard. Even when they would rather just sweep it under the rug. Peacemakers understand that sometimes, the cost of not addressing an offense or a miscommunication is steep and could end important relationships. They prioritize their relationships over being right and understand that even when they seek peace, it's possible the relationship may not be reconciled. Yet as far as it depends on them, they pursue peace, regardless of the outcome.

On the other hand, peace-takers are those who deny offenses and miscommunication. They specialize in sweeping stuff under the rug. They cringe at the thought of healthy communication because it might mean they have to discuss something hard. They are great at being the victim because then they don't have to take any responsibility for the strained relationship. Peace-takers lack humility, maturity, and integrity.

Bathsheba was obviously a peacemaker. Instead of succumbing to a victim mentality, she took her new life circumstances by the reins and put on her big-girl panties. We don't know the details of this process, but if we look at the facts of her story, we can probably piece it together.

Bathsheba was treated unfairly—an extreme understatement, I know. She was impregnated by David. Her husband was killed. She became David's seventh wife. Her child died a week after birth. And all of this happened within a nine-month time period.

It's likely she felt unseen and forgotten by God. However, through the birth of Solomon and God's provision, I suspect healing began to take place. When we go through hard stuff, like Bathsheba did, it's sometimes a challenge to remember our suffering won't last forever. God knows we can't take a lifetime of pain, and in His grace and mercy He always provides in ways that confirm His goodness. It's through this goodness that we start trusting Him fully, which leads to transformation and peace.

When our relationships are at peace, we likely won't be faced with much drama. However, there are two kinds of peace: inner peace and peace with others. These two kinds of peace complement and influence each other. For example, if we don't have strong inner peace, then it's very likely our relationships with others will suffer, thus creating a lack of peace in our lives in general. Likewise, our inner peace can be influenced by the state of our external relationships. If our relationships are in a state of disarray, then we all know it can mess with our own inner peace.

One of the biggest challenges peacemakers face is not necessarily a lack of desire for peace but rather confusion on how to have hard conversations and walk through conflict in a way that honors God. In my book *Heart Sisters*, I share the PEG system for conflict resolution. The PEG system is an acronym to help us know what to do when we feel like we might need to have a difficult conversation:

> **P**ray
> **E**xamine your role
> **G**o and talk with the other person

Let's consider each step. The first is to pray. So often, we are tempted to involve other people, but this isn't what God wants us to do. God wants us to seek Him first. If we seek others first, we are involving people who may not need to be involved, and this can toe the gossip line pretty quickly. And listen, I understand how difficult this can be. It's natural to desire confirmation that we've been wronged, but we have to remember that perception is different for everyone. When we are feeling a catch in our spirit about an offense, miscommunication, or misunderstanding, our first step should be to pray and ask God for wisdom in the situation. It's also important to ask Him to reveal our part in the conflict and any sin we may have committed. Humility is critical when having a difficult conversation with someone else. In fact, it's very likely the factor that will determine if the relationship is reconciled or destroyed.

The next step is to examine your role. When we are in the examination stage, it's helpful to think about these six questions:

- What is my role in this conflict?
- Am I hurt because of my own insecurity?
- Am I expecting too much, and are my standards too high?
- Will I be able to spend time with the person who hurt me without thinking about it?
- Will I be able to trust this person again?

After we assess our answers to these questions and we feel we need to discuss the situation with the other person, then the next step is to go and talk with the person involved. I like how *The Message* explains Matthew 18:15: "If a fellow believer hurts you, go and tell him—work it out between the two of you. If he listens, you've made a friend." In other words, we are supposed to work through conflict with only the other person involved.

I recently discovered an ancient personality assessment called the

Enneagram, which has become popular in Christian circles. The Greek word *ennea* means "nine" and the word *gram* means "points." The Enneagram organizes nine different dominant personality types on a circular figure and, without getting into too much detail, teaches us how unique and different from one another we all really are. Learning about the nine types of the Enneagram has been a game-changer for me because it's allowed me to understand how each of us is motivated and how everyone perceives the world. Embracing and understanding our differences—while also allowing one another to be the people God created us to be—are key components of living in peace with others.

When it comes to our own pain and suffering, we are often wounded by relationships, but we are healed by relationships as well. Some of our deepest pain comes at the hands of other people, as we saw with Bathsheba and David. As I've already mentioned, I recently experienced a friend betrayal, and it was excruciating. I was definitely wounded by this relationship. However, God brought lovely new friendships into my life that are safe, authentic, and fortifying, thus offering me healing and hope at a time when I needed it most. Even though I was wounded by a relationship, I've been healed through relationships as well.

But truth be told, after experiencing such hurt, I wanted to retreat and never offer my heart to another in friendship again. I needed time to lick my wounds and work through my pain with God, and while doing so, I realized to live in isolation is exactly what the enemy would want after we've been wounded. Yes, it's wise to be cautious with our hearts. But it's not wise to keep our hearts isolated and alone because that's how we become vulnerable to the lies that threaten to derail us.

It's sad when relationships end. Actually, it's just downright heartbreaking at times. I once heard an adage claiming that some people will be friends for a reason, some will be friends for a season, and some will be friends for a lifetime. I'm always amazed by the friends who I think are lifetime friends but end up being season friends, and vice versa. It's really only our relationship with Jesus that is promised and certain to never be taken away. He will never change. He is the same as He was yesterday and will be the same tomorrow. We will change and grow as we continue in the process of sanctification, but He never will. However, we hold our earthly relationships in open palms and strive for peace—as much as it depends on us.

Turning to God

Prayerfully read and meditate on the following Scriptures:

Proverbs 18:24
Ephesians 4:2-3
Hebrews 10:24-25

Questions for Reflection or Discussion

1. Reflect on the difference between peacemakers and peace-takers. Has your perception of peacemakers changed at all? Why do some think of peacemakers as doormats? What do you think God would say about those who are peace-takers? Why?
2. Read Hebrews 10:24-25. What does Paul suggest we do for one another? Why is it important to live in community and not isolation?
3. Reflect on your own relationships. Have you ever seen the end of a friendship? What did you learn through this process? How did you heal? What do you look for in a friend now versus before?
4. Ephesians 4:2-3 are two of my favorite verses of the Bible. Read these verses in the New Living Translation and *The Message* on Biblegateway.com or another Bible translations website. Why do we need to be patient with one another? What do we need to do when there is conflict?
5. Proverbs 18:24 in *The Message* says, "Friends come and friends go, but a true friend sticks by you like family." This is much like "friends for a reason, friends for a season, friends for a lifetime." Reflect on these. What has been your experience with this?
6. How do you think the PEG system can help resolve conflict?

Would you add anything to this model? Why is it important to God that His followers live in peace?

7. Bathsheba seemed to know a thing or two about peace because she acclimated to her new life well and seemed to find a peace from God regarding her situation. What can we learn about choosing peace from Bathsheba? Is Bathsheba a doormat, or is she a wise woman who knows when to speak and when to listen? Do you think Bathsheba valued peace? Why or why not?

11

Forgiving Others—and Yourself

Forgiveness is not an occasional act. It's a constant attitude.

—Martin Luther King Jr.

*F*orgiveness is an integral part of our healing journey, just as it must have been a big part of Bathsheba's story. We can't fully understand how she transformed and became the woman of courage and hope we see in 1 Kings 1 without talking about forgiveness.

Have I mentioned that I have a strong sense of right and wrong? A justice-seeker of sorts? And I like for justice to be served when there has been an offense? Also, another fun fact: my husband and all three of my children are as well. Justice-seekers have strong beliefs of what is right and wrong and will not hesitate to speak up in the face of injustice. This sounds really great on paper, and when channeled well, it's a wonderful quality. However, not everyone shares the same opinion of what is right and wrong. In our family, everyone gets one hill to die on a day. If someone starts to get riled up, I simply pose the question, "Is this your hill?" and, depending on the answer, the passion is either diffused, or we move on to the next step. It's a sight to behold. It's very possible all three of my children may start their own law firm together someday and actually get paid for what they do best.

Anne Lamott once said, "Not forgiving is like drinking rat poison and then waiting for the rat to die."[1] In other words, when we refuse to forgive, we're the ones who are damaged, not the one who has offended us. When we choose not to forgive, bitterness, resentment, and anger eat away our souls like battery acid. Yet, this is not the message we get about forgiveness from our culture.

We live in a world where it's normal to seek revenge. An eye for an eye. Don't get mad, get even. Seek your own justice. The list goes on because our world tends to stress revenge and getting even more than forgiveness and turning the other cheek. We're also often taught that forgiveness is not for our benefit; it's for the person who caused us pain. We can lord it over them until we decide they're worthy of our forgiveness. But this isn't how God sees forgiveness at all.

First of all, forgiveness is not for the person who wrongs you; *it's for you*. Countless studies have been conducted on the effectiveness of forgiveness therapy. When those who have been hurt are led by a counselor through a forgiveness-based approach to healing, clients report greater peace, life satisfaction, and contentment. Choosing to forgive reinstates a sense of control for the one who suffers and allows forgiveness to occur, even if the offender hasn't asked. I once thought I didn't have to forgive someone unless they asked for forgiveness, but that's just another lie our culture perpetuates. My lack of forgiveness actually interfered with my own healing, and the one who caused my pain wasn't affected at all. I drank the rat poison and waited for the rat to die.

While we are again left to "fill in the blanks" of Bathsheba's healing, we can see evidence of forgiveness in her relationship with David in 1 Kings 1. While she certainly didn't choose to be a survivor of his sin, that's where the unexpected turn in her life led. She chose peace in the face of adversity, and in doing so she very likely arrived at the point of forgiveness for David. When Bathsheba approaches King David in

1 Kings 1, commentaries suggest David and she had a more casual or familiar relationship and a very strong bond.[2] When we walk through difficult times with someone else, it can either knit your souls together or tear them apart. Because it seems as if the tragic loss of their son knit David's and Bathsheba's souls together and they had a genuine love and understanding of each other in the end.

I think we also have to recognize that God forgave David even after he had committed several hurtful sins that affected other people's lives. Because God knew David's heart, He understood that David loved Him but had been deceived and disillusioned by sin because he's human. God's grace and mercy extended to David and therefore likely encouraged Bathsheba to forgive David as well. Forgiveness begets forgiveness.

While we know this sounds really good in theory, forgiveness isn't always tied up with that nice Christian bow everyone seems to like so much. Let's just be real, friend: forgiveness is hard work. I know because—full disclosure—I'm not always so great at forgiveness. I'm moving in the right direction, but as someone who is a justice-seeker, I sometimes prefer to go for that eye-for-an-eye goal instead.

The problem with this? It's not how God wants us, as His people, to respond. Our heart and flesh may fail, but our God never will. Which is good because if there's ever a time when we need His guidance, it's when we are navigating the deep waters of forgiveness.

Scripture has much to say about forgiveness, but I think we can find the bottom line in 1 John 1:9-10. I like the New Living Translation: "But if we confess our sins to him, he is faithful and just to forgive us our sins and to cleanse us from all wickedness. If we claim we have not sinned, we are calling God a liar and showing that his word has no place in our hearts."

Without humility, there will be no confession. A humble spirit before God is what leads us to His forgiveness.

Now, you know how I love to look at other translations of the same verses, so let's look at what *The Message* has to say:

> If we claim that we're free of sin, we're only fooling ourselves. A claim like that is errant nonsense. On the other hand, if we admit our sins—make a clean breast of them—he won't let us down; he'll be true to himself. He'll forgive our sins and purge us of all wrongdoing. If we claim that we've never sinned, we out-and-out contradict God—make a liar out of him. A claim like that only shows off our ignorance of God.

God will forgive us of our sins and purge us of all wrongdoing. Yes, please. It's so great to be on the receiving end of grace, isn't it? But then, we turn around and read this: "Instead, be kind to each other, tenderhearted, forgiving one another, just as God through Christ has forgiven you" (Ephesians 4:32 NLT).

Forgiveness begets forgiveness. In other words, since God has forgiven us of so much, we are expected to forgive those who hurt us as well. If we receive grace, we're expected to also give it away. Grace-receivers must also be grace-givers.

There's another person who needs to receive your grace—you. God expects us to extend grace to ourselves as well. When I was twenty-three years old, I committed a sin that broke my heart. I lived with the shame of this sin for years and was terrified of anyone ever finding out what I had done. I asked God for forgiveness almost daily until one day, it was clearly placed on my heart that He had forgiven me the first time I confessed. Continually asking for His forgiveness only demonstrated my own lack of faith and belief that He is who He says He is. Soon after, I realized it was time to forgive myself as well. Accepting God's forgiveness but not forgiving myself felt like a form of pride. If God can forgive me, then why can't I forgive myself? I'm certainly not above God, and yet He offers me His grace. It was time to stop carrying that heavy mantle of shame and walk in freedom. I now speak candidly about my sin of choosing to have an abortion in the hope it will save lives in the future.

I think before we embark on a journey of forgiveness, we also have to be clear on what forgiveness is not. As I said before, we are so often inundated with false information regarding forgiveness, so let's clear some of this up. First of all, when we forgive someone who has hurt us, we are not excusing or condoning their behavior. We are also not pretending we aren't hurt. So often, we respond with, "It's OK!" to an apology when in actuality it's never OK to hurt another person. A better response is, "Thank you for your apology. I forgive you." Accepting an apology doesn't excuse bad behavior. It excuses the stronghold unforgiveness can have on your soul.

Forgiveness also doesn't mean the offender should immediately be trusted again. It's very possible that someone who has hurt us can earn our trust again if they repent and possess true humility, which is likely what happened between David and Bathsheba. However, this is a process, and the offender cannot expect trust to magically occur after the apology has been delivered. When an apology is offered for the offender's benefit, it's called false humility; and since God knows our hearts, we can't keep our motivations hidden from Him. He can spot false humility quicker than immediately.

Forgiveness also isn't always a "one and done" thing. Sometimes, we have to repeatedly choose to forgive for the same offense. There will come a day when we won't have to do so anymore; however, especially at the beginning of the forgiveness journey, we may have to choose to forgive more often. And while this is sometimes true of forgiveness in our earthly relationships, thankfully, God doesn't have to keep forgiving us for the same offense. As we read in 1 John 1:9-10, if we are humble and confess our sins, we're forgiven. Boom. Just like that. God's forgiveness is one and done. Aren't you just so grateful for this?

In the end, forgiveness is a process and a journey. Interestingly enough, recent research has indicated that we need to be careful not to force someone who has been wounded to forgive too early in the grieving process.[3] Forcing forgiveness too early can lead to the survivor doing so for external approval rather than for authentic healing. This, in turn, could actually be a detriment to their healing process. This confirms what we discussed in chapter eight—that is, it's important to give someone who is suffering the space to sit in their grief and begin the forgiveness process when they start to feel ready. It's true that sometimes action precedes emotion; however, in the case of trauma survivors, this isn't usually true.

Forgiveness also has many layers. For example, my father was a severe alcoholic. When I became an adult, I had to forgive his alcoholism. Then I had to forgive his abandonment. Then the adultery that occurred because of his intoxication. Eventually, I landed at a place of peace and was able to see my father as a kind, gentle, very broken man who was strapped by an addiction so fierce that his entire life was derailed. I'm so thankful forgiveness allowed us to have a relationship before he passed away almost twenty years ago.

Lastly, forgiveness doesn't mean reconciliation will occur. It only takes one to forgive, but it takes two to reconcile. In other words, we don't have to wait for our offender to seek our forgiveness because forgiveness is our choice. We can choose to forgive them even before they ask. Or if we are the offender, we can seek forgiveness, but we can't force who we hurt to forgive us. Likewise, we can desire reconciliation after an offense, but we can't make someone be in a relationship with us. In fact, in the case of abuse, it isn't usually a good idea for a survivor to reconcile with his or her abuser unless the abuser has been completely rehabilitated and the survivor chooses to reconcile.

Once upon a time long ago, I ran the Chicago Marathon. Every time I think of the forgiveness journey, it reminds me of running that marathon. After the first mile, I wanted it to be over. I could have quit, but then I had trained so hard. So really, the only option was to keep running. There were miles when it felt easy, like maybe I wasn't as crazy as I thought I was to willingly run 26.2 miles. And there were miles that felt like every inch was painful, when I considered limping over to the tents at each mile marker for those who just didn't think they could go on. Through the grace of God, I kept going, but when I reached mile 22, I had another rough moment. Four miles feels like 50 when you've already run 22. Just as the tears were springing forth, a man who was well into his seventies sidled up to me and said, "Just keep running. You can do this. Finish strong." Then he sprinted away. Crossing that finish line is still, to this day, one of my greatest accomplishments.

Friend, just keep going. You can do this. Finish strong. Forgiveness is a marathon as well because it's a journey we travel with a sometimes-rough terrain. Sometimes, we will want to quit because we don't think we can go on. Sometimes, it will feel like we've got this. And sometimes we'll wonder what we were thinking to willingly offer forgiveness at all. Thankfully, God places encouragers along the way, just like the older man who offered some inspiration up to me when I needed it the most. When you have crossed the forgiveness finish line, the accomplishment will be great, the fruit will be sweet, and your strength will not be shaken. You've got this.

Turning to God

Prayerfully read and meditate on the following Scriptures:

Psalm 91
Psalm 103:12
2 Corinthians 5:17

Questions for Reflection or Discussion

1. Think about how our culture portrays forgiveness. Discuss with your group or reflect on your own how these misconceptions can hinder our healing. What truths about forgiveness can replace the lies we often hear?
2. Reflect on Psalm 91. What hope does this offer you? What promises does God make?
3. How can forgiveness set us free? How can it keep us in chains? How is forgiveness like a marathon?
4. Read 2 Corinthians 5:17. How does this offer us hope after we have sinned? Does it offer you hope? Why or why not? How could this encourage Bathsheba?
5. What does Psalm 103:12 say about what God does for us?
6. What role do you think forgiveness played in Bathsheba's own healing? How did forgiveness give her the confidence she needed to approach David about making Solomon the rightful heir to the throne?

$\approx$ **12** $\approx$

Turning to Hope

And the God of all grace, who called you to his eternal
glory in Christ, after you have suffered a little while,
will himself restore you and make you strong, firm and
steadfast.

—1 Peter 5:10

*A*t speaking engagements I often talk about women's
friendships, and Bathsheba is one of seven women of
the Bible I lift up as types of friends we need in our lives.
There are always a handful of women who approach me afterward to
express how they identify with her. I describe Bathsheba as a woman
who has been through some stuff and lived to tell about it—not only
lived but thrived. I'd love to share a meal with her and learn from her,
wouldn't you? I imagine her possessing a stoic wisdom and generous
love, much like poet Maya Angelou or author Toni Morrison. I hope
by now you've caught a love for this amazing woman of the Bible and
the message behind her story.

Let's recap what we've seen so far. Bathsheba was forced to sleep
with King David, which resulted in pregnancy. Then David tried to
cover up his sin by enticing her husband, Uriah, to go home and sleep
with his wife. When Uriah refused, David had him moved to the front
line of battle where, of course, he was killed. When he was confronted

by Nathan, David repented and sought God's forgiveness, but the consequences still remained. Bathsheba and David's son died seven days after his birth, confirming that David's sin took him farther than he had ever planned to go.

When David comforted Bathsheba after the death of their son, they conceived Solomon. At some point, David promised Bathsheba that Solomon would be his successor. But Adonijah, the next oldest living son, assumed it should be him and tried to usurp the throne right out from under Solomon. As we see in 1 Kings 1, Bathsheba boldly confronted her husband with his promise and persuaded him to reinstate Solomon as the rightful heir.

Since it's not specifically mentioned in Scripture, we don't really know the depth of Bathsheba's healing. However, we see the quality of her character in the wisdom and courage she used to confront David. It's possible this wisdom and courage developed as a result of combatting shame, anger, comparison, and fear through self-care and God's love. This could have led her to embrace peace and forgiveness, thus guiding her on how to choose to respond to her grief.

It also seems as though David greatly respected Bathsheba until his death as evidenced when he called her back into the room and proclaimed Solomon as the rightful heir in 1 Kings 1:28-29. In addition, she crowned Solomon when he married the Queen of Sheba (Song of Songs 3:11), and she was given a seat of honor in his throne room (1 Kings 2:13-21). As we also see in these scriptures, like his father, King Solomon loved and revered his mother. Interestingly, Proverbs 31:28 says, "Her children arise and call her blessed; her husband also, and he praises her." Many speculate that author of Proverbs 31 is none other than Bathsheba herself.[1]

Just when you thought you had heard all the good about our heroine, there's more—and this is big. Are you ready for this? Bathsheba is one of only five women specifically mentioned in the genealogy of Jesus.

Jesus is one of Bathsheba's descendants. The King of Kings, Savior, Son of God, Messiah—right from Bathsheba's bloodline.

When I first started studying the Bible, I used to gloss over the geneology sections because I didn't quite understand the significance, and, truth be told, I found them to be a little dry. However, I now understand the significance of detailing the lineage of Jesus. Matthew 1:1-17 begins the New Testament with a detailed list of the lineage of Jesus. Most verses include the names of the men of Jesus's bloodline; however, Tamar, Rahab, Ruth, Bathsheba, and Mary, mother of Jesus, are the only women mentioned in the genealogy of Jesus.

Genesis 38 tells the story of a young woman whose husband dies at a young age. As per Israeli custom, the brother of the deceased husband must bear children with his brother's wife if they had not yet had children; however, this did not happen. After being denied a second husband, Tamar took matters into her own hands and dressed as a prostitute, convinced her father-in-law to hire her for the evening, and tricked him into conceiving twin boys, one of which is an ancestor of Jesus. Tamar was bold and courageous even if she was a little deceptive.

In Joshua 2, we meet Rahab, a prostitute living in the town of Jericho. Rahab courageously agreed to house two Israelite spies who were gathering information about an upcoming attack on the town. As a result, Rahab and her family were spared during the battle. She later married Salmon and gave birth to a son named Boaz. Rahab was bold and courageous, even if she was a prostitute.

In the Book of Ruth, we meet Naomi, the mother of two sons married to Ruth and Orpah. Following the deaths of her husband and both sons, Naomi orders her daughter-in-laws to return to their homelands so they can find new husbands (Ruth 1:11-13). Ruth, understanding this would mean a life of destitution and possibly death for Naomi, refused to leave her behind. Instead, she traveled to Bethlehem with Naomi and met Boaz, a wealthy landowner. Ruth and

Boaz eventually married, and Naomi was provided for for the rest of her life. Ruth gave birth to Obed, father of Jesse, who was the father of David. Like Tamar and Rahab, Naomi was bold and courageous and did what she had to do to survive.

Matthew 1:6 says, "David was the father of Solomon, whose mother had been Uriah's wife." We know Uriah's wife, though not specifically named, is Bathsheba. Our heroine. The woman who fell victim to circumstances beyond her control and, as a result, lost her husband in battle and a son. Who, at one point, had everything, and in the blink of an eye, she had nothing. The woman who is often portrayed as an adulteress. The woman who later boldly stood up for what was right and restored the throne to it's rightful heir. Bathsheba was bold and courageous and redeemed.

Mary, mother of Jesus, is the last woman mentioned in Matthew 1:16. Mary was a very young woman betrothed to Joseph and was chosen by God to be the mother of Jesus. A young woman who had to face the possibility of being stoned (as the punishment for adultery in Israel during biblical times was stoning) and ostracized for becoming pregnant outside of marriage. Mary was bold and courageous and trusted God even when His plan didn't quite make sense to her.

Do you notice a theme with these five women? With the exception of Mary, all of these women were broken. A deceptor. A prostitute. A young widow. A victim of power. They all likely understood the meaning of fear. Yet each of these women was chosen because God knew the level of courage they possessed could get the job He had called them to do done. And they did. These are the women from whom Jesus descends.

Why is it important to understand from whom Jesus descends? Because God wants us to understand He will use anyone, regardless of their track record. Doesn't that just fill you with hope to know that God will take you just as you are and use you for a great purpose? None of these women, or men for that matter, were perfect. Yet God!

I am confident Bathsheba was not having fun when her life took a very unexpected turn because of David's sin. Things certainly didn't go as planned, and I'm also certain there were tenuous moments during her healing journey. Yet her story is a beautiful testimony of God's promise to make beauty from ashes. Bathsheba and David produced five sons, the most famous being King Solomon; and God knew all along that His own Son, Jesus, would be a direct descendent of Bathsheba's. If that doesn't send chills up and down your spine, I don't know what will.

Even after finishing this book, I don't think any of us will be thrilled to find pain and suffering knocking on our door. However, I pray we all have deeper hope after reading and contemplating Bathsheba's story. I read somewhere that when we are in the midst of a trial, we must remember that it's not a period; it's a comma. A period is final while a comma means a continuation. As long as we are still here, our pain and suffering is a comma, not a period. There may be pain in the night, but joy comes in the morning (Psalm 30:5).

If you are currently in a valley of pain and suffering, remember this season in your life is a comma. I will not minimize your grief, because you may need to sit in it for a while, and that's OK as long as you don't stay there forever. I will not advise you to forgive right now, because, for authentic and transformative forgiveness, you need to forgive when your heart is ready. And I will not tell you everything will always be just fine, because there will be periods of our lives that won't feel just fine. I once heard Jennifer Rothschild share something at a speaking engagement that affected me profoundly. She said, "It may not be well with my circumstances, but it can be well with my soul." We can't always control our circumstances, much like Bathsheba. However, we can choose how we react, and if by God's grace we choose that our soul will be well, it will be well—no matter what.

If you've ever researched pain and suffering in the Bible, then you've likely read James's words found in the first chapter of his book.

I like James because he didn't mince words. He shot straight and didn't sugarcoat much, so there wasn't a lot of mystery to his messages. Here's what he had to say about pain and suffering: "Consider it pure joy, my brothers and sisters, whenever you face trials of many kinds, because you know that the testing of your faith produces perseverance. Let perseverance finish its work so that you may be mature and complete, not lacking anything" (James 1:2-4).

Again, we may not really consider it pure joy when we face trials. But I think we can all agree that the testing of our faith produces perseverance—and perseverance leads to maturity and completion, which sounds great to us all. Paul said something very similar in his letter to the Romans:

> Now that we have been made right with God by putting our trust in Him, we have peace with Him. It is because of what our Lord Jesus Christ did for us. By putting our trust in God, He has given us His loving-favor and has received us. We are happy for the hope we have of sharing the shining-greatness of God. We are glad for our troubles also. We know that troubles help us learn not to give up. When we have learned not to give up, it shows we have stood the test. When we have stood the test, it gives us hope. Hope never makes us ashamed because the love of God has come into our hearts through the Holy Spirit Who was given to us. (Romans 5:1-5 NLV)

Troubles help us learn not to give up, and when we have learned not to give up, we have stood the test. Standing the test leads to hope. And hope, like the kind I see in Bathsheba's story, is what gives us the strength to keep climbing out of the valley—because there's a reward to be had. You'll see.

Turning to God

Prayerfully read and meditate on the following Scriptures:

Isaiah 61
Romans 5:1-5
James 1:1-4

Questions for Reflection or Discussion

1. Read the above verses in the New Living Translation. What stirs in your soul when you read? Now read the same in the *The Message*, noticing again what stirs your soul. What is different between the versions? Is there one that speaks to you more than the other? Why or why not?
2. What has inspired you the most about Bathsheba's story? Why? What have you learned from her?
3. Think about a time when you've had to persevere. What was the end result? How do perseverance and hope go hand-in-hand?
4. Why do you think God planned for Jesus to descend from the line of Bathsheba? What is signficiant about her being part of His genealogy?
5. What are your top three take-aways from reading *The Bathsheba Battle*? Why? How will this apply to your daily life?
6. Do you think the geneology of Jesus is important? Why or why not? What other qualities do you notice Tamar, Rahab, Ruth, Bathsheba, and Mary have in common? How do you think God viewed these women?
7. Proverbs 31 contains advice from a mother (Bathsheba) to her son (King Lemuel, who was believed to be King Solomon[2]). Read through these passages. Are there any that stand out to you now that you know Bathsheba's story? Which verses speak to you right now?

We hope you enjoyed *The Bathsheba Battle*. Want more from Natalie? Here is an excerpt from her previous book *Heart Sisters*.

HEART SISTERS

Becoming the Friend You Want to Have

NATALIE CHAMBERS SNAPP

ABINGDON PRESS | NASHVILLE

CHAPTER ONE

BUT DO WE REALLY *NEED* GIRLFRIENDS?

The glory of friendship is not the outstretched hand, nor the kindly smile nor the joy of companionship; it is the spiritual inspiration that comes to one when he discovers that someone else believes in him and is willing to trust him.

Ralph Waldo Emerson

I've always wanted to have a sister. For as long as I can remember, I longingly watched the girls who had built-in playmates to share giggles with in the middle of the night and inside jokes about Uncle Harry at family reunions. As an only child, I would have taken a brother as well, but a sister? Oh, the desire of my heart was strong. In fact, I still find myself feeling like an outsider looking in to blood-sister relationships during those moments when I forget I do indeed have sisters—though not by blood.

Through His grace, God granted me those sisters years later. No, we don't have a shared childhood and we don't have inside jokes during family reunions. However, we do have heart connections that only sisters can have, and the love I possess for these women rivals the love I have for my husband and children. You mess with one of my sisters and the pit bull of my usually even-keeled self starts to smack its jowls.

After becoming a follower of Christ when I was twenty-seven years old, I quickly put the pieces together that it is He who creates us as women to be relational beings. Listen, I love my husband something fierce, but let's face it—there are some things the men in our lives are just not going to understand. And who are we kidding? They don't *want* to understand everything.

During our newlywed years, I told my husband more than he ever wanted to hear. I gave him the whole book when what he really wanted was the summary on the back cover. I lost him early and found myself offended when he only listened to 70 percent of the story because I wanted 100 percent of his attention. Similarly, my husband understands why our two young sons, who are fifteen months apart, have the desire to catapult themselves off the top bunk of their beds because he once was a young boy who wanted to do the same thing. He is; therefore, he knows. Meanwhile, my daughter and I look on, befuddled yet accepting that we'll never quite understand, while at times the boys look at us in the same way.

Now, let's change the scenario to one of my closest friends and me in a booth at our favorite Mexican joint munching on chips and salsa and talking over the same situation I shared with my husband. Invariably, my friend wants to hear more of the story. She might ask guiding questions or offer solutions or points to ponder from a female perspective because women typically get other women. This doesn't mean our husbands don't "get" us—there's just a different level of understanding between two women who both know what it's like to have lost yourself amid the diapers and feedings or the carpooling or the pressure to balance it all. Don't get me wrong—our husbands can also be incredibly insightful and sensitive to our thoughts and feelings. I'm in no way bashing the male species.

However, the truth of the matter is we need other women in our tribe. We need to lean on one another and hold each other up when it feels like we can't walk. We need someone to lovingly tell us we should apologize to our spouses when we're in the wrong. We need someone to speak up if the dark brown lipstick makes us look like a corpse. Simply put, God knew we would need all kinds of relationships to fulfill the desire He placed in each of our hearts to live in community.

When we expect our husbands, or any man for that matter, to fulfill all of our relational needs, we are placing an enormous amount of pressure upon his shoulders. If we keep expecting him to fulfill the role of girlfriend, husband, and in some cases, God, we are setting that man up for failure. It's just not realistic nor is it fair to expect him to be able to meet every one of those needs. (And if you have the courage to read the former sentence out loud to your husband, tell him I said "you're welcome.")

So let's consult the Bible and dig around a bit, shall we? Evidence of women-as-relaters is found throughout the Bible beginning with the creation of Eve. God created Adam but soon realized there was "no suitable helper" (Genesis 2:20). After placing Adam in a deep sleep, God created Eve from one of Adam's ribs and he awoke to find the bone of his bone and the flesh of his flesh. No small feat, and of course, he suddenly had the suitable helper he needed. If only it were always so simple, eh?

Eve was created to commune with Adam. The mother of us all was made from his very being to interact and relate to Adam, the first man on the planet. It's a good thing she seemed to like him—she didn't have much else of a choice! Besides this, she became his "help meet" (Genesis 2:20 KJV) and apparently did so pretty effectively since eventually Cain and Abel were born. There might have been a little dysfunction since Cain eventually killed Abel, but then we can rest assured knowing that even the first family on earth had a little baggage.

There's no way around it, sisters. We are who we are who we are. We can't expect the cat to start barking. We are relationship seekers and we were created to be so.

Ruth refused to leave Naomi. Mary immediately sought Elizabeth after learning she was carrying the Christ child. Esther used her relational understanding to stop the destruction of the Hebrews. The list continues but, suffice it to say, there are several examples of women as relaters throughout the Bible.

However, it's not just the Bible that demonstrates the importance of women as relaters. In a landmark study from UCLA roughly ten years ago, it was discovered that when women feel stressed, their brains release a hormone called oxytocin.[1] Oxytocin makes women want to surround themselves with other women, and this releases even more oxytocin, which has a relaxing effect and makes us think everything might be all right after all.

Left over from a time when humans had to be more aware of their surroundings in order to live, the fight-or-flight response describes our natural inclination to flee the scene if we feel threatened. However, the research that coined this phrase was conducted mostly on men. The same UCLA study referenced above found that women and men actually respond to stress differently. (Which, I might add, I didn't need an official study to know. Throat clear.)

In her book *The Tending Instinct*, Shelley E. Taylor discovered that when women feel stressed, they "tend and befriend."[2] In other words, after a tough day, we like to spend the evening tending to our children and befriending our sisters around us. Let the oxytocin gates open and may the flooding begin, I say. The more oxytocin released, the calmer we feel. Hook me up to an intravenous drip, please.

Our bodies even respond *biologically* when we spend time with girlfriends, thus explaining why a night out with the girls now and then is essential to our sanity. Likely due to the oxytocin release, several studies have found social relationships are helping us to live longer, too. Those who have a strong friendship network find themselves with lowered cholesterol, heart rate, and blood pressure. Harvard University is even in on this as well—in their well-respected *Nurses' Health Study*, they discovered that a woman without a network of friends posed a risk to her health that was comparable to smoking or carrying around extra weight.[3] Sobering facts indeed. Girlfriends are a lifeline we cannot afford to live without.

The Bible not only includes several examples of women as strong and pivotal relational beings but also showcases a few women who chose not to live in such a sisterly manner as well. Leah and Rachel, who were blood sisters nonetheless, lived in a state of constant jealousy and rivalry with one another. Jacob was tricked into marrying Leah, a woman he found unattractive but who was so fertile she bore him six sons and one daughter. Yet Jacob didn't love her in the way he loved her sister, Rachel.

> *Looking sideways at what others have instead of looking up to God and thanking Him for what He's already given you never leads to anything good.*

It was Rachel he wanted all along because she was a knockout of a woman, but get this—she was infertile. In fact, Rachel was so bent on bearing sons for Jacob she offered up her maidservant, Bilhah, who bore him two sons. No wonder the twelve tribes of Israel came from Jacob's lineage—he was one prolific breeder.

Some scholars believe that Leah's "weak eyes" refer to the fact they were likely crossed or disfigured in some way. Though her beauty may not have won her the Miss Israel title, she possessed the good eggs that conceived several sons, which eventually led to six of the tribes of Israel. Rachel wanted nothing more than to bear Jacob sons, and Leah wanted nothing more than to obtain Jacob's love. They both desperately wanted what the other possessed. Looking sideways at what others have instead of looking up to God and thanking Him for what He's already given you never leads to anything good. The story of Jacob's wives was the perfect storm—and to think some people believe the Bible is an outdated history book. This trio's story is juicier than any episode of *Days of Our Lives* I've ever seen; not to mention their dilemma is one that continues among women today.

Another example of strife between women in the Bible is Sarai and Hagar. Like Rachel, Sarai (later renamed Sarah) was unable to conceive a child with her husband, Abram (later renamed Abraham). Also like Rachel, she offered up her maidservant, Hagar, to Abram, who lay with her and conceived a son. Soon after, Hagar began to resent Sarai, and Sarai quickly blamed Abram for putting her in this position. (Can you just picture a befuddled Abram trying to figure this one out?) Evidently, he was ready to wash his hands of this situation as he gave Sarai permission to do as she liked with her maidservant. Sarai's solution was to simply be so horrible to Hagar that the only thing the poor maidservant could do to alleviate this tense situation was to flee her mistress.

And flee she did. Hagar ran, confused and alone and desperate to know what God's plan was for her. God spoke to Hagar while she was retrieving water at a well during her journey, and after instructing her to go back to Sarai with the promise He would give Hagar too many descendents to count, He said:

> You are now with child
>   and you will have a son.
> You shall name him Ishmael,
>   for the LORD has heard of your misery.
>
> He will be a wild donkey of a man;
>   his hand will be against everyone
>   and everyone's hand against him,
> and he will live in hostility
> toward all his brothers.
> (Genesis 16:11-12)

Ishmael later became the patriarch of Islam. The repercussions of a fallen female relationship know no boundaries, and its impact can go further than you ever imagined. I'm pretty sure Sarai had no idea of the generational impact her impatience with God's timing would produce.

And, yes, I know there are women who have been horribly wounded by other women. I understand why some women desire to just be left alone or count only men among their friends. One of my readers, who we'll call Stephanie, confided in me she's only recently had girlfriends because she was betrayed and deeply hurt by a friend while in college. This particular friend shared personal information about Stephanie with others—information that had been shared in confidence and was tender to Stephanie's heart. Doesn't this just make you think of the phrase "with friends like these who needs enemies?"

Stephanie retreated from female relationships and became very selective of whom she would give a glimpse into her vulnerabilities. She became a "surface friend" to many but didn't have any friends who truly knew her heart. Stephanie found women to be catty and petty and preferred the company of men.

However, as we discussed earlier, men are equipped to only go so far into the heart of a woman because at the end of the day, they're not women. Being just one of the guys might work for a little while, but eventually, there are going to be situations where a female heart will desire friendship with other women. Our spouses can't be expected to be our sisters. Luckily, Stephanie was able to work through this past hurt, and today has been rewarded with true Heart Sisters who love her and can completely be trusted.

It doesn't help that our culture seems to glorify and profit from catty behavior either. The whole "Real Housewives of Wherever" series is fraught with behavior between women that actually encourages us to live in strife with one another. In fact, the cattier and more disrespectful the behavior among the women on these types of programs, the higher the network ratings. It's true that a story of conflict naturally piques our interest as those disabled by the flesh, but what would happen if we just simply refused to watch shows like "The Real Housewives of Wherever"?

If we waste our time being catty instead of caring, we are extinguishing the light the Holy Spirit illuminates within us.

As followers of Jesus, it's our responsibility to monitor what we allow to enter our hearts. If we do indulge in a guilty pleasure, balancing it out with what is true, noble, pure, and just will keep our hearts centered on God. Television, books, magazines, and websites impact us more than we know. It's our job to guard our hearts *above all else,* and this includes monitoring what we allow into our souls. Caring is always better than catty.

If we waste our time being catty instead of caring, we are extinguishing the light the Holy Spirit illuminates within us. While teaching the Sermon on the Mount in Matthew 5, Jesus talked to the crowd around Him about being the salt and the light. He often taught in parables, stories told with a simple lesson or moral. These intentional parables always had a specific focus, and Jesus knew the direction He was heading and the lessons He wanted His listeners to glean. I admit to being a bit befuddled when I first read about the salt and the light because come on . . . I can purchase salt in a cylinder at my local grocery store for about a dollar. How valuable is that?

Turns out, very. In ancient times, salt was thought to be extremely rare and quite valuable. It was often used as currency, was the culprit of a few conflicts, and according to Homer, was a "divine substance."[4] Salt was set apart. Precious. Not to mention there are more uses for salt than just seasoning our food or melting the ice on our roads. In fact, the salt industry claims fourteen thousand different uses for these small pieces of the only consumable rock in existence.[5] Salt can be used to remove stains from clothing, brighten up the colors of vegetables, seal cracks, extinguish grease fires, and kill poison ivy, to name a few.

In other words, salt is not only precious and valuable. It's useful. And we're called to be the "salt and the light"—which means we are precious, valuable, and useful.

Salt also naturally brings out better flavor in what we eat and preserves food from spoiling; therefore, we are to bring out the better flavor in others and keep them from spoiling. In this way, we are useful to God. In the NET Bible, Jesus tells us, "You are the salt of the earth. But if salt loses its flavor, how can it be made salty again? It is no longer good for anything except to be thrown out and trampled on by people" (Matthew 5:13). Is it just me or does this make you a little concerned about losing your flavor? And yes, there are days in which I feel like I've lost my flavor. There are certainly moments when I feel as if God might want to throw me out. Luckily, God's grace covers those less-than-favorable moments.

So we're called to be the salt, which means we are to be set apart. We're precious, valuable, and useful. But we're also called to be the light. Like salt, there is a certain power in light we so often take for granted. Light allows us to function after the sun goes down. It makes scary moments feel not as frightening when it's turned on. It produces a comforting glow. Figuratively, light illuminates the secrets we want to keep in the darkness, so the enemy can't prowl around them anymore. Light is powerful, illuminating, reduces fear, and encourages truth.

It's a bit of a tall order, sisters. If we're called to be the salt and the light, then we're asked to be set apart, precious, valuable, useful, powerful, illuminating, fear-reducing, and truth-seeking. As Jesus shares, "You are the light of the world. A city located on a hill cannot be hidden. People do not light a lamp and put it under a basket but on a lampstand, and it gives light to all in the house. In the same way, let your light shine before people, so that they can see your good deeds and give honor to your Father in heaven" (Matthew 5:14-16 NET).

Let your light shine, sisters. Don't dim it because of fear or because you're worried about someone else's insecurity or are too worried about what others will think of you. Allowing your light to shine is a true example of loving your neighbor as yourself. Loving the women in your life through your sincere and loving light is what Jesus asks us to do. Shine bright.

Now that we've reviewed this background a bit, here's where guarding our hearts is relevant: the eyes are the lamp of the body. We draw light into ourselves through our eyes, and the light that shines out to the world comes from the same place. Therefore, what we allow our eyes, or our lamps, to see is going to affect the kind of light that illuminates those around us—and usually without us even realizing it's happened. What goes in certainly does come out, and unfortunately, I know this from experience.

Years ago, I spent a few months only reading *People* magazine and the latest bestsellers. I would not have dreamed of missing the weekly episode of *The Bachelor*, and I wasn't keeping up with my typical daily reading of the Bible. Soon, I found myself thinking catty thoughts about other women.

Camaraderie was replaced by competition as I began to look at the exterior instead of the heart. I even began to compare my very boring life to those in magazines, books, and television. So I can't help wondering what I am subconsciously illuminating to the world around me if I watch television shows that encourage cattiness among women. How does the media influence how I treat women in my sphere of influence?

Recently, I've been drawn to the book of Matthew, and since I'm using a relatively new translation called The Voice in conjunction with the New International Version, I am discovering connections between Scriptures I haven't seen in the past. In The Voice translation, Matthew 7:13-14 tells us

> *there are two paths before you;*
> *you may take only one path.* One
> doorway is narrow. *And one door*
> *is wide.* Go through the narrow
> door. For the wide door leads to
> a wide path, and the wide path
> is broad; the wide, broad path is
> easy, and the wide, broad, easy
> path has many, many people
> on it; but the wide, broad, easy,
> crowded path leads to death.
> The narrow door leads to a nar-
> row road that in turn leads to life.
> It is hard to find that road. Not
> many people manage it.

Not many people manage it because it's far easier to walk the wide path the world so freely offers. However, if we choose to take the narrow path and learn about Jesus, the narrow is suddenly more enticing. I'm not suggesting that trials and heartbreak are suddenly erased once we start to walk the narrow path, but as a hammer helps us pound nails into a board, the narrow path gives us the tools we need to stay on the narrow path. Shoot your arrow toward the narrow path and hide from the wide.

Matthew 22:37-40 tells us that the first and greatest commandment is to love God with all our hearts, souls, and minds. The second is to simply love your neighbor as yourself. Every single teaching in the New Testament is based on these two— one called the "Great Commandment" and the other the "Great Commission." There's something about that word "commandment" that makes me think we should probably just do it. Likewise, when we commission someone, we hire that person. We've been hired by God to do the specific job of loving others as ourselves. Jesus didn't suggest we choose to follow these two principles, and He didn't ask if we wanted to do so. He commanded and commissioned it. He's not messing around with these two.

To shoot our arrow toward the narrow path, we need to choose to love God above all else and then choose to love those around us as ourselves. Choosing to love the women around us and desire good for them is an example of loving our neighbors as ourselves. We rejoice when they rejoice and we weep when they weep (Romans 12:15).

We are all broken. Every last one of us. Each of us has days in which we are ministering to others and days when we are being ministered to. He wants us to be in the game. He needs us to show up and be the hands and feet of His son. It's our job.

What could happen if we started a revolution of love, support, and sisterhood among women? How much freedom would we feel if we gave each other the benefit of the doubt and chose relationship instead of conflict? Would our hearts break less if we chose to work through those conflicts in humility instead of running away and adding more layers to the scars? Would we fight the inappropriate media that stereotypes us as catty and against one another and force it to stop? Would extramarital affairs even exist if women agreed to stand together as sisters? The power we have as women is staggering.

We need someone to share in our laughter. Sometimes we need a good cry with a sister by our side. Other times, we need her to carry us because we simply don't think we can put one foot in front of the other on our own. We need Heart Sisters.

Notes

1. University of California Los Angeles, "UCLA Researchers Identify Key Biobehavioral Pattern Used by Women to Manage Stress," Science Daily, www.sciencedaily.com/releases/2000/05/000522082151.htm.
2. Shelley E. Taylor, *The Tending Instinct* (New York: Henry Holt, 2002), 21.
3. Gale Berkowitz, "UCLA Study of Friendship Among Women," www.scribd.com/doc/16043143/Ucla-Study-on-Friendship-Among-Women.
4. John Mariani, "Shaking Up the Salt Myth: This Thanksgiving, Go Ahead and Pour on the Sodium Chloride," *New York Daily News*, November 24, 2011, www.nydailynews.com/opinion/shaking-salt-myth-thanksgiving-pour-sodium-chloride-article-1.982027.
5. SaltWorks, "Salt Uses and Tips," www.saltworks.us/salt_info/salt-uses-and-tips.asp.

Acknowledgments

J've always said that writing a book is like giving birth; and when we are preparing to have a child, a team of people are often involved. Likewise, a team of people are always involved in the writing of a book. There are so many I would like to thank for their assistance in writing about the story of Bathsheba, which I'm so passionate about sharing.

First and foremost, God. Oh, God. You continually amaze me. Thank you for entrusting me to write a little bit about one of your beloved daughters from long ago whose story is still so relevant.

Thank you, Jason Snapp, for always telling me to "go for it"—even when, like Moses, I try to think of every reason why I shouldn't. You help me get out of my own way, and I am so grateful. Thank you, also, for picking up the family management slack when I was writing under a tight deadline.

I am forever grateful to the amazing Pamela Clements, who saw the beauty in *Heart Sisters* and first gave me the chance to start writing books after blogging for so many years.

Sally Sharpe, I adore you for so many reasons. You "get" me and never try to push me to be someone or something I'm not. Thank you for your enthusiasm and support. You are the best editor ever, ever. You make my writing sound so much better.

Thank you, Jamie Chavez, for reading these words and offering your opinions and insights. You are a fabulous editor as well and, like Sally, have made this book even better.

My children, Sarah, Samuel, and Spencer, help me grow as a person daily. If you ever want to expediate your sanctification process, then get married and have kids. You three are my joy, my light, my eternal loves.

Karri Huckstep, you know I stand in awe of you. Everyone does. You are one amazing woman. Thank you for sharing your heart in this book so that those who have not had the honor of meeting you can still learn from your wisdom.

Lastly, thank you to Beth and Dave Booram, for opening a place such as the Fall Creek Abbey, where I can hole away for four days and write five chapters of a book. Your gift of hospitality is evident, and your kindness provided comfort as I was in crazy-writer mode. Thank you.

Notes

Introduction

1. Becky Hughes, "Remembering Billy Graham: His Most Powerful Quotes on Life and Spirituality," *Parade*, February 21, 2018, https://parade.com/648000/beckyhughes/remembering-billy-graham-his-most-powerful-quotes-on-life-and-spirituality/.

2. *Merriam-Webster*, s.v. "heal," www.merriamwebster.com/dictionary/heal.

1. Getting Real

1. Margery Williams Bianco, *The Velveteen Rabbit: or How Toys Become Real* (Leesburg, VA: GiGi Books, 2003).

2. Understanding Your Pain and Suffering

1. "Half of Everyone Will Experience Trauma. Here's How To Grow from It," Big Think, https://bigthink.com/big-think-mental-health-channel/one-half-of-everyone-experiences-trauma-heres-how-to-grow-from-it.

2. Robert Burns, "To A Mouse," in *Poems, Chiefly in the Scottish Dialect* (Philadelphia, PA: Patterson and Cochran, 1798), 122.

3. "About the CDC-Kaiser ACE Study," Centers for Disease Control and Prevention, www.cdc.gov/violenceprevention/childabuseandneglect/acestudy/about.html.

4. Turning Away from Shame

1. Brene Brown, *The Gifts of Imperfection: Let Go of Who You Think You're Supposed to Be and Embrace Who You Are* (Center City, MN: Hazelden, 2010), 38.

2. Brene Brown, *Daring Greatly: How the Courage to Be Vulnerable Transforms the Way We Live, Love, Parent, and Lead* (New York: Gotham, 2012), 64.

5. Turning Away from Anger

1. Christian Nordqvist, reviewed by Timothy J. Legg, "How Can I Control My Anger?" *Medical News Today*, last updated December 19, 2018, www.medicalnewstoday.com/articles/162035.php.

2. Karen Ehman, *Keep It Shut: What to Say, How to Say It, and When to Say Nothing At All* (Grand Rapids: Zondervan, 2015), 20.

6. Turning Away from Comparison

1. Kendra Cherry, "Social Comparison Theory in Psychology," Verywell Mind website, updated January 11, 2019, www.verywellmind.com/what-is-the-social-comparison-process-2795872.

2. University of Pennsylvania, "Social Media Use Increases Depression and Loneliness, Study Finds," ScienceDaily website, updated November 8, 2018, www.sciencedaily.com/releases/2018/11/181108164316.htm.

3. Honor Whiteman, "Social Media: How Does It Affect Our Health and Well-Being?" *Medical News Today*, updated June 10, 2015, www.medicalnewstoday.com/articles/275361.php.

7. Turning Away from Fear

1. Jason Soroski, "Just Drop the Blanket: The Moment You've Never Noticed in *A Charlie Brown Christmas*," Crosswalk.com, updated December 14, 2015, www.crosswalk.com/special-coverage/christmas-and-advent/just-drop-the-blanket-the-moment-you-never-noticed-in-a-charlie-brown-christmas.html.

8. Permission to Grieve

1. Anna Swartz, "Elephant Herd Comforts Grieving Mom Over Loss of Her Calf," The Dodo website, January 7, 2015, www.thedodo .com/elephant-herd-comforts-grievin-918372088.html.

9. The Mind-Body Connection

1. Mike Mazzalongo, "Penitential Psalms," BibleTalk TV, posted May 24, 2017, https://bibletalk.tv/penitential-psalms.

11. Forgiving Others—and Yourself

1. Anne Lamott, *Traveling Mercies: Some Thoughts on Faith* (New York: Pantheon, 1999), 134.

2. Jessica Feinstein, "Bathsheba Is One of the Most Beguiling Characters of the Bible," *U.S. News*, January 25, 2008, www.usnews .com/news/religion/articles/2008/01/25/bathsheba-is-one-of-the -most-beguiling-characters-in-the-bible.

3. Gayle Reed and Robert Enright, "The Effects of Forgiveness Therapy on Depression, Anxiety, and Posttraumatic Stress for Women After Spousal Emotional Abuse," *Journal of Counseling and Clinical Psychology* 74, no. 5 (2006): 920–29.

12. Turning to Hope

1. Dalaina May, "What You Need to Know About Bathsheba," The Junia Project, April 28, 2015, https://juniaproject.com/what-you -need-to-know-bathsheba-in-new-light/.

2. May, "What You Need to Know About Bathsheba."

About the Author

Natalie Chambers Snapp is an author, blogger, and speaker known for her refreshing authenticity and practical approach to life and God's Word. She describes herself first as a follower of Jesus, then wife to Jason, and mom to one spunky daughter and two spirited sons with a whole lot of energy. Not choosing to follow Jesus until the age of twenty-seven, she is passionate about sharing the grace, mercy, and truth of God's love with others "regardless of your track record." Her transparency and humor endear her to women of all ages.

Natalie is the author of the book *Heart Sisters: Be the Friend You Want to Have* and *Becoming Heart Sisters: A Bible Study on Authentic Friendships*. She has written for various blogs and online devotionals, including Proverbs 31 and Group Publishing. Natalie is pursuing a master's in counseling so that she may be better equipped to help broken people find healing through her writing and speaking. She lives in the Midwest with her crew where she writes about faith in everyday life from mundane to chaos and everything in between.

Follow Natalie:

- 🐦   @NatalieSnapp
- 📷   @nataliesnapp
- 📘   @AuthorNatalieSnapp
- Blog   NatalieSnapp.com (check here for event dates and booking information)